ADVENTIST International COOKBOOK

Favorite vegetarian recipes from kitchens

around the world

DEBBY SHABO WADE

Pacific Press® Publishing Association

Nampa, Idaho

Oshawa, Ontario, Canada

Edited by: Aileen Andres Sox
Cover globe illustration and inside design: Michelle C. Petz

Library of Congress Cataloging-in-Publication Data

Wade, Debby, 1951–
    Adventist international cookbook : favorite vegetarian recipes from kitchens
around the world / Debby Shabo Wade.
        p. cm. — (The Adventist kitchen)
    ISBN 0-8163-1780-1
    1. Vegetarian cookery. 2. Cookery, International. I. Title. II. Series.
TX837.W14297 2000
641.5'636—dc21
                                                    99-087770

Contents

Dedication 4

Inroduction 5

SECTION 1: Drinks 7

SECTION 2: Breads 23

SECTION 3: Salads 38

SECTION 4: Entrees 54

SECTION 5: Vegetables . . .100

SECTION 6: Desserts 116

SECTION 7: Miscellaneous
        Soups, sauces, dips 138

Glossary 155

Index 156

Dedication

To three special ladies who have contributed to my life:
My mom, who as a single parent patiently supported and encouraged me as I began cooking at age 7;
my sister Becky, who learned with me;
(I'm glad we survived the gas oven blowing up in our faces when we tried our first cake recipe!)
And Aunt Barbara, who never said anything about the fudge on her ceiling
after the double boiler I tried to make from two pans exploded *(of course I tried to hide the evidence).*
I love you all.

Introduction

My interest in learning to prepare foods from different countries and cultures probably started when I was a home economics major at Walla Walla College. I'll never forget one of the classes I took from Mary Schwantes. I'd bring home "taste treats" from around the world and try them out on my new husband. Some of them made a hit. But others only made him roll his eyes and question how anyone could eat such a thing. (I didn't include any of the eye-rollers in this book!)

Through the years I've picked up a lot of recipes from friends. When we lived in the Washington, D.C. area, we attended Capital Memorial Church, and one of the biggest events every year was the International Vegetarian Meal sponsored by our multi-cultural congregation. Hundreds of people from the community would make reservations and come to one of the sittings for this popular event. I made sure I got around to all the tables to sample what was available—and ask for recipes!

When our family lived in Singapore for several years, we developed a taste for many Indian, Chinese, Malaysian, Indonesian, and Thai dishes that we probably never would have encountered otherwise. I had fun trading cooking lessons with women from these various countries, teaching them how to make American-style bread in exchange for lessons on the finer techniques of preparing their national cuisines.

Since returning to the U.S., I've had a chance to try out many of these recipes on American guests. I've adapted a few of the recipes to make them a little more American in style, but for the most part, I've presented the recipes just as the original cooks shared them.

So, you're about to embark on an international adventure, as you try these yummy vegetarian recipes. You'll probably need to add some new items to your spice shelf, and I've suggested where you can get ingredients that aren't in supermarkets. You might be tempted to pass by something as simple and common as Pinto Beans, but don't. I got that recipe from my friend at Pacific Press, Loida Morales, because I could never figure out how she made her beans taste so rich and creamy without adding a lot of extra fat.

Speaking of fat, most of the recipes (except the desserts!) are naturally low in fat and calories, so I haven't included low-calorie versions as I did in the *Adventist Potluck Cookbook*. But in a few recipes, I have suggested substitutions that can lower the calorie count. If you're concerned about cholesterol, you can always use an egg replacer product in place of the eggs.

I hope you enjoy these recipes as much as I do. One thing's sure: As you try out these recipes from around the world, your family will never again accuse you of just serving the "same old same old" stuff all the time!

Happy international cooking!

SECTION 1

Drinks

A TASTE OF THE TROPICS

Fruit Cooler

Makes 16 servings

24 ounces frozen orange juice concentrate
4 bananas
2 quarts ice cream,* softened
1/2 teaspoon ground nutmeg

In a blender, process orange juice and bananas until smooth; put into a one-gallon container. Add softened ice cream and nutmeg; stir well. Add enough water and ice to bring the measurement up to one gallon. Serve.

*LITE VERSION SUBSTITUTION: To lower fat, calories, and cholesterol, substitute a flavored frozen yogurt for the ice cream.

PER SERVING

Calories:	227
Total Fat:	7 g
Cholesterol:	30 mg
Sodium:	59 mg
Carbohydrates:	39 g
Protein:	4 g

☆Orange Cooler

Makes 16 servings

1 1/4 cups canned pineapple juice
3 bananas
2 1/2 quarts frozen orange juice concentrate
3 ounces frozen lemonade concentrate

In a blender, process pineapple juice and bananas. Pour into a one-gallon container; add remaining ingredients. Add enough ice to bring the measurement up to one gallon. Serve.

**A TASTE OF
THE TROPICS**

PER SERVING

Calories:	110
Total Fat:	0.2 g
Cholesterol:	0 mg
Sodium:	2 mg
Carbohydrates:	27 g
Protein:	1 g

Raspberry Lemonade Cooler

Makes 12 servings

40 ounces frozen raspberries, thawed
1 6-ounce can frozen lemonade concentrate, thawed
2 quarts ginger ale, chilled

In a medium saucepan over medium heat, cook raspberries for 8 minutes. Strain through a fine strainer, pushing the back of a spoon into berries to release the juice. Save juice, discard seeds. Cool.

In a large juice container, mix raspberry juice and lemonade concentrate. Add chilled ginger ale; serve in glasses filled with ice.

PER SERVING

Calories:	173
Total Fat:	0.2 g
Cholesterol:	0 mg
Sodium:	13 mg
Carbohydrates:	45 g
Protein:	0.7 g

Lemon & Lime Barley Water

Makes 4 servings

8 cups water
1 cup pearl barley
1/4 cup bottled lemon juice
1/2 cup bottled lime juice
1/2 cup granulated sugar

A TASTE OF EUROPE

In a large kettle over medium-high heat, boil barley in water for 30 minutes, or until liquid has reduced by half. Remove from heat; strain into a colander, saving water. Discard barley.

Pour barley water into a small pitcher. Add lemon juice, lime juice, and sugar; mix well. Serve chilled with ice. Garnish with lemon or lime slices.

PER SERVING

Calories:	108
Total Fat:	0.1 g
Cholesterol:	0 mg
Sodium:	18 mg
Carbohydrates:	29 g
Protein:	0.2 g

NORWAY

Christmas Wassail

Makes 12 servings

1 1/2 cups granulated sugar	1 tablespoon ground ginger
4 cups water	1 cinnamon stick
3 whole allspice	1 1/3 cups reconstituted orange juice
6 whole cloves	2/3 cup lemon juice concentrate

In a large kettle over medium-high heat, combine sugar and 2 cups boiling water; bring to a boil. Turn off heat. Add spices; cover. Set aside for 1 hour to steep. Strain mixture; pour back into kettle. Add remaining water and fruit juices; bring to a boil again. Serve hot or cold.

PER SERVING

Calories:	131
Total Fat:	1 g
Cholesterol:	0 mg
Sodium:	15 mg
Carbohydrates:	33 g
Protein:	0.6 g

Curried Tomato Juice

ROBIN RUSSELL

A TASTE OF SOUTHERN ASIA

Makes 8 servings

1 46-ounce can low sodium tomato juice
1 tablespoon margarine
1 teaspoon vegetarian Worcestershire sauce
2 1/2 teaspoons curry powder

In a medium saucepan over medium heat, melt margarine. Add curry powder; stir well. Add tomato juice and Worcestershire sauce; stir. Heat and serve.

SERVING SUGGESTION: You can chill this drink as well. If you like it spicier, add more curry powder.

PER SERVING

Calories:	43
Total Fat:	1 g
Cholesterol:	0 mg
Sodium:	39 mg
Carbohydrates:	7 g
Protein:	1 g

FRANCE

French Hot Chocolate

Makes 16 servings

2/3 cup semisweet chocolate chips
1/2 cup light corn syrup
1/4 cup + 2 tablespoons water
1 teaspoon vanilla extract
2 cups whipping cream*, chilled
8 cups skim milk

In a small saucepan over low heat, melt chocolate chips in corn syrup, and water; stir constantly. Stir in vanilla. Remove from heat; place in refrigerator to chill.

In a medium, chilled bowl, whip cream until stiff. Add chilled chocolate mixture gradually to whipped cream, beating until mixture mounds when dropped from a spoon. Refrigerate.

Before serving, heat milk in a large kettle over medium heat. *Do not boil.* Fill mug 1/2 cup full with whipped cream mixture. Add milk slowly until mug is full. *You can either blend in the cream mixture with a spoon, or let it sit on top.* Serve while hot.

PER SERVING

Calories:	219
Total Fat:	14 g
Cholesterol:	43 mg
Sodium:	82 mg
Carbohydrates:	20 g
Protein:	5 g

*Lite Version Suggestion: To cut down on cholesterol, you could try using fat-free whipped topping in place of the whipping cream.

Glögg (GLUHG)

Makes 6 servings

3 cups water
1 3-ounce package orange-flavored gelatin
1 cinnamon stick
6 whole cloves
3 orange slices

In a medium saucepan over medium-high heat, dissolve gelatin in boiling water. Turn heat off; add cinnamon stick, cloves, and orange slices. Cover; let stand for 5 minutes. Remove spices and oranges. Pour mixture into mugs; serve hot. Garnish with a cinnamon stick or orange slices.

SWEDEN

PER SERVING

Calories:	123
Total Fat:	1 g
Cholesterol:	0 mg
Sodium:	56 mg
Carbohydrates:	29 g
Protein:	2 g

RUSSIA

Russian Tea

Makes 44 servings

2 cups orange-flavored drink mix, sweetened

1 1/4 cups granulated sugar

1/2 cup decaffeinated instant tea powder
   (sweetened or unsweetened)

1 teaspoon ground cinnamon

2 packages lemonade powder, sweetened

1/2 teaspoon ground cloves

In a large bowl, mix all ingredients together. Store in an airtight container in a dry place. When ready to use, measure 2 1/2 teaspoons or 1 tablespoon into a mug; add 8 ounces of boiling water.

A variation of this popular recipe can be found in the **Adventist Potluck Cookbook.**

PER SERVING

Calories:	66
Total Fat:	0 g
Cholesterol:	0 mg
Sodium:	3 mg
Carbohydrates:	17 g
Protein:	0.1 g

Spiced Tea

Makes 20 servings

1 cup granulated sugar
1 cup water
12 whole cloves
2 cinnamon sticks
3 decaffeinated tea bags

2 quarts water
3/4 cup frozen orange juice concentrate
1/2 cup lemon juice concentrate
1 cup canned pineapple juice

ENGLAND

In a large pot over medium-high heat, combine sugar, 1 cup water, cloves, cinnamon, and tea bags; bring to a boil. Remove from heat; cover. Allow to steep for 30 minutes. Strain out cloves, cinnamon, and tea bags. Add remaining 2 quarts water, orange juice, lemon juice, and pineapple juice. This can be served hot or cold.

PER SERVING

Calories:	68
Total Fat:	1 g
Cholesterol:	0 mg
Sodium:	14 mg
Carbohydrates:	17 g
Protein:	0.5 g

INDIA

Mango Lassi

Makes 5 servings

1 fresh mango, seeded and peeled
2 cups plain yogurt
10 ice cubes
1 to 3 tablespoons granulated sugar

In a blender, blend all ingredients on high speed until smooth.

So refreshing and yummy.

SERVING SUGGESTION: Lassis are great with a spicy meal. Serve with one of the curries in this book.

PER SERVING

Calories:	91
Total Fat:	3 g
Cholesterol:	12 mg
Sodium:	47 mg
Carbohydrates:	13 g
Protein:	4 g

Sweet Lassi

Makes 4 servings

2 cups plain yogurt
10 ice cubes*
3 tablespoons granulated sugar

In a blender, blend all ingredients at high speed until smooth.

How easy can you get—my husband can even manage this recipe!

INDIA

* If you like a thicker shake, add a few more ice cubes; if you prefer it thinner, leave out a few ice cubes.

PER SERVING

Calories:	111
Total Fat:	4 g
Cholesterol:	16 mg
Sodium:	59 mg
Carbohydrates:	15 g
Protein:	4 g

A TASTE OF EUROPE

Frosty Yogurt Drink

Makes 6 servings

3 1/2 cups skim milk, chilled
1 6-ounce can frozen orange juice concentrate, thawed
1/3 cup honey
1/3 cup instant decaffeinated tea powder
1 cup plain yogurt, chilled

In a blender, blend milk, orange juice, honey, tea, and yogurt until smooth and frosty. Pour into glasses. Serve with a fresh mint leaf.

PER SERVING

Calories:	149
Total Fat:	1 g
Cholesterol:	8 mg
Sodium:	96 mg
Carbohydrates:	28 g
Protein:	7 g

Seth's ☆Orange Sensation

SETH WADE

Makes 4 servings

4 ounces frozen orange juice (do not thaw)
3/4 cup 1% milk
3/4 cup water
1/2 teaspoon vanilla extract
2 tablespoons granulated sugar
1 cup crushed ice

In a blender, process all ingredients on high speed. Serve immediately.

Really is refreshing!

PER SERVING

Calories:	90
Total Fat:	0.6 g
Cholesterol:	2 mg
Sodium:	25 mg
Carbohydrates:	19 g
Protein:	2 g

**A TASTE OF
THE TROPICS**

Banana-Grape Smoothie

Makes 4 servings

4 ripe bananas, peeled
2 cups grape juice

Freeze bananas: Store two bananas in a zip-lock baggy to freeze. *If you store more than two bananas together, it is difficult to break them apart once they have frozen.*

In a blender, process grape juice and frozen bananas until smooth. Serve immediately.

This drink is a must to try because it is so refreshing and it uses up all those overripe bananas that you don't have time to make into banana bread!

VARIATIONS: Use any type of juice to create your own flavors and interesting colors as well. Have fun. If you want a thicker smoothie, use more banana; thinner, leave out one banana.

PER SERVING

Calories:	182
Total Fat:	0.7 g
Cholesterol:	0 mg
Sodium:	5 mg
Carbohydrates:	45 g
Protein:	2 g

Breads

FRANCE

Breakfast Muffins

Makes 15 muffins

1/3 cup shortening
1/2 cup granulated sugar
1 egg
1 1/2 cups unbleached flour
1 1/2 teaspoons baking powder
1/2 teaspoon salt

1/4 teaspoon ground nutmeg
1/2 cup 1% milk
1/2 cup granulated sugar
1 teaspoon ground cinnamon
1/2 cup butter, melted

In a large bowl, cream shortening, 1/2 cup sugar, and egg either by hand or with an electric mixer. While mixing add flour, baking powder, salt, nutmeg, and milk; mix until smooth. Fill greased muffin pans 1/2 full with batter *(these are tea-type muffins, so you don't want to fill the muffin tins too full)*. Bake at 350°F for 20 to 25 minutes.

In a small bowl, mix 1/2 cup sugar and cinnamon; in a separate bowl, melted butter. After removing muffins from oven, remove from pan and dip into butter, then roll in cinnamon sugar. Serve hot.

PER SERVING

Calories:	200
Total Fat:	11 g
Cholesterol:	31 mg
Sodium:	178 mg
Carbohydrates:	23 g
Protein:	2 g

Banana Scones

Makes 18 scones

2 cups unbleached flour	2 tablespoons butter, melted
1/2 teaspoon salt	1/2 cup mashed banana
3 teaspoons baking powder	1 egg
1/4 cup granulated sugar	2 tablespoons milk

In a medium bowl, combine flour, salt, baking powder, and sugar. Add butter.

In a small bowl, beat together banana, butter, egg, and milk. Make a well in the flour mixture; pour liquid into it. Stir gently with a fork until moistened. Drop mixture onto a greased cookie sheet by spoonfuls. Bake at 400°F for 12 to15 minutes, until golden brown. Serve plain or with butter.

**A TASTE OF
THE TROPICS**

PER SERVING

Calories:	84
Total Fat:	2 g
Cholesterol:	15 mg
Sodium:	137 mg
Carbohydrates:	15 g
Protein:	2 g

ENGLAND

Scones

Makes 8 scones

2 cups unbleached flour	1/3 cup butter
3 teaspoons baking powder	1/3 cup buttermilk
1 teaspoon salt	1 egg (separate 1 tablespoon egg white)
2 tablespoons granulated sugar	Granulated sugar (to sprinkle)

In a medium bowl, combine flour, baking powder, salt, and 2 tablespoons sugar. Cut in butter with a pastry blender until the mixture resembles coarse meal.

In a small bowl, add buttermilk to egg (reserve 1 tablespoon egg white). Beat until blended; pour into dry ingredients, stirring to moisten. Turn out dough onto a lightly floured counter. Pat lightly and use rolling pin to roll out 3/4" thick. Use a biscuit cutter, or cut into squares or triangles.

In a small bowl, beat remaining egg white and 1 teaspoon water until frothy; brush onto scones. Sprinkle with granulated sugar and bake at 425°F on an ungreased cookie sheet for 10 to 15 minutes, until golden brown.

SERVING SUGGESTION: Serve with marmalade or currant jam. The English eat their scones with clotted cream (see glossary).

PER SERVING

Calories:	207
Total Fat:	8 g
Cholesterol:	47 mg
Sodium:	499 mg
Carbohydrates:	28 g
Protein:	4 g

Chapatis

Makes 12 servings

2 cups whole wheat flour
1/2 teaspoon salt
3/4 cup water (approximately)

INDIA

In a medium bowl, combine flour and salt. Add enough water to form a firm dough. On a lightly floured surface, knead dough for 5 minutes. Place dough back into bowl; cover. Let rise one hour. Divide dough into 12 balls; roll out thinly on a lightly floured surface.

In a greased skillet over medium-high heat, place chapatis one at a time. When chapati bubbles and is lightly browned, turn. Brown the other side, pressing flat with a pancake turner.

PER SERVING

Calories:	68
Total Fat:	0.4 g
Cholesterol:	0 mg
Sodium:	1 mg
Carbohydrates:	14 g
Protein:	3 g

INDIA

Traditionally, naans are slapped onto the side of a tandoor or clay oven to bake.

Naan

Makes 10 servings

2 teaspoons dry yeast
4 teaspoons warm water (112°F)
2 teaspoons granulated sugar
4 cups unbleached flour
1 teaspoon baking powder
1/2 teaspoon salt
2/3 cup milk

2/3 cup plain yogurt
1 egg
1 tablespoon ghee* or margarine
Flour, for dusting
Ghee or margarine, for greasing
Chopped cilantro (optional)
Onion seeds (optional)

In a small bowl, let yeast, warm water, and sugar stand until foamy.

In a medium bowl combine milk, yogurt, egg, ghee or margarine, salt, baking powder, and 1 cup flour. Beat together with yeast to work up the gluten. Add enough flour to be able to knead dough on a smooth surface for 8 to 10 minutes. Place dough in a greased bowl; cover. Let rise until doubled. Punch down; divide dough into 10 balls.

Roll out each ball on a smooth surface into 10" x 6" ovals. Transfer onto greased cookie sheets and brush melted ghee or margarine over dough; sprinkle with cilantro and onion if desired. Bake at 400°F 10 to 12 minutes, until golden. Serve warm with curry and rice.

I like to make a dipping sauce out of plain yogurt and fresh, chopped cilantro. What great flavors!

*See glossary for definition.

PER SERVING

Calories:	227
Total Fat:	3 g
Cholesterol:	29 mg
Sodium:	167 mg
Carbohydrates:	41 g
Protein:	7 g

Pita Bread [Khobiz]

JAMES, JR. AND LISA WEISHAAR

Makes 12 pitas

2 1/2 teaspoons dry yeast
1 teaspoon granulated sugar
1/4 cup warm water
1 1/2 to 2 cups unbleached flour

1 1/2 cups whole wheat flour
1 teaspoon salt
1 teaspoon olive oil
1 cup warm water

A TASTE OF THE MIDDLE EAST

In a small mixing bowl, dissolve yeast and sugar in 1/4 cup water and let stand until foamy.

In a deep bowl, combine flours and salt; make a well in the center. Pour yeast mixture, oil, and remaining 1 cup water into well. Using your hand, gently blend the ingredients in the depression, then begin incorporating the flour. Continue mixing and kneading in the bowl for about 10 minutes, until a smooth dough results. *(Add a little more flour or water if necessary to achieve this.)* Cover with a clean towel. Let rise until doubled.

Preheat oven to 475°F. Place the dough on a lightly floured board; knead with floured hands for 5 minutes. Tear off pieces the size of oranges; roll between cupped hands to form smooth balls. Set balls aside on a floured cloth; cover. Let rise for 30 minutes.

Sprinkle baking sheets with cornmeal. Using a rolling pin, roll out each piece of dough into a circle about 1/4" thick. Arrange the circles on the baking sheets, cover with a towel; let rise again for 30 minutes. Place baking rack on the lowest rung of the oven; let pitas bake for 5 minutes, until they puff up and are lightly browned.

PER SERVING

Calories:	134
Total Fat:	1 g
Cholesterol:	0 mg
Sodium:	180 mg
Carbohydrates:	27 g
Protein:	4 g

A Jewish Tradition

Challah is the traditional braided Jewish Sabbath loaf. This yeast bread is delicious cooled, but even better eaten warm from the oven, with pieces torn rather than cut from the loaf.

The Challah one sees in bakeries is often made from six strands of dough. To have a loaf symbolic of the Sabbath, you need seven strands (one strand for each day of the week). The loaf is made of three small interwoven strands atop three large interwoven strands. These are crowned by a single strand, signifying the Sabbath—the crown of the week.

The number of strands does not affect the flavor or texture of this very satisfying bread. You might want to make three-, four-, or six-strand braids during the week, and bake a loaf of seven strands Friday to greet the Sabbath on Friday night.

Challah

Makes 20 servings

2 teaspoons dry yeast	1 egg
1/4 cup warm water (112°F)	1 tablespoon shortening
1/2 teaspoon granulated sugar	2 1/2 cups unbleached flour
1/2 cup warm water	1 egg yolk
2 1/2 teaspoons granulated sugar	2 tablespoons cold water
1 teaspoon salt	

ISRAEL

In a small bowl combine yeast, 1/2 teaspoon sugar, and 1/4 cup warm water; let stand until foamy.

In a medium bowl, stir yeast mixture, 1/2 cup warm water, 2 1/2 teaspoons sugar, salt, 1 egg, shortening, and 1 1/4 cups flour; beat until smooth. Mix in enough remaining flour to be able to turn out on a floured smooth surface and knead for 8 to 10 minutes. Place dough in a clean, greased bowl; cover. Let rise until doubled. Punch down; divide into 3 equal parts.

Roll each part into 14 inch strands. Place strands closely together on a lightly greased cookie sheet; braid together. *Do not stretch.* Fasten ends and tuck under. Let rise until doubled. Heat oven to 375°F. Beat egg yolk and cold water; brush over braid. Bake 25 to 30 minutes, until golden brown.

SERVING SUGGESTION: Serve with Mushroom-Walnut Spread (see p. 152).

PER SERVING

Calories:	69
Total Fat:	1 g
Cholesterol:	11 mg
Sodium:	111 mg
Carbohydrates:	13 g
Protein:	2 g

ENGLAND

English Muffin Loaf

Makes 32 servings

5 1/2 cups unbleached flour
2 tablespoons dry yeast
1 tablespoon granulated sugar
2 teaspoons salt

1/4 teaspoon baking soda
2 cups 1% milk
1/2 cup warm water
Cornmeal (for sprinkling)

In a large bowl, combine 3 cups flour, dry yeast, sugar, salt, and baking soda.

In a small saucepan, heat milk and water until very warm (120 to 130°F). Add to dry mixture; beat well. Stir in enough flour to make a stiff batter. Spoon into 2 well-greased loaf pans that have been sprinkled with cornmeal. Sprinkle top of batter with cornmeal and pat down evenly. Let rise for 45 minutes. Bake in a preheated oven at 400°F for 25 minutes. Remove and allow to cool on wire racks.

This bread is great for toast when sliced!

PER SERVING

Calories:	88
Total Fat:	0.4 g
Cholesterol:	1 mg
Sodium:	142 mg
Carbohydrates:	18 g
Protein:	3 g

Focaccia (foh·KAH·chee·ah; Americans tend to pronounce it foh·KAH·sha)

ITALY

Makes 20 servings

2 teaspoons dry yeast
2 tablespoons warm water (112°F)
1/2 teaspoon granulated sugar
1 cup water
1 1/2 teaspoons salt

2 3/4 to 3 cups unbleached flour
1 tablespoon olive oil
1 teaspoon dried basil
1/2 teaspoon dried oregano

In a small bowl, combine yeast and 2 tablespoons warm water. Add sugar; stir. Let stand till foamy.

In a medium bowl, combine 1 cup water, yeast mixture, salt, and flour. *(Add enough flour to make a stiff dough.)* Turn out onto floured surface; knead 8 to 10 minutes, adding enough more flour as needed until dough is smooth and elastic. Place dough in a greased bowl; cover. Let rise until doubled. Punch down; divide dough into two balls.

Roll balls into 8" circles on two greased cookie sheets; cover. Let rise until doubled. Preheat oven to 375°F. Gently push depressions into the dough with your fingertips. Evenly distribute 1/2 tablespoon olive oil over each circle; sprinkle 1/2 teaspoon dried basil and 1/4 teaspoon dried oregano over each circle. Bake for 20 to 25 minutes.

There are many things you can do with focaccia bread. You can use it for a pizza crust or serve it just as it comes out of the oven along with your favorite pastas. Yum!

PER SERVING

Calories:	76
Total Fat:	1 g
Cholesterol:	0 mg
Sodium:	161 mg
Carbohydrates:	14 g
Protein:	2 g

MEXICO

Green Chili & Onion Bread

BARBARA MITZELFELT

Makes 32 servings

1/4 cup warm water	1 tablespoon salt
5 teaspoons dry yeast	1 teaspoon cup granulated sugar
1 teaspoon cup granulated sugar	1/4 cup margarine
1 cup lowfat cottage cheese	1 4-ounce can diced green chilies
2 eggs	1 large onion, chopped
1/4 teaspoon baking soda	5 cups unbleached flour

In a small bowl, combine water, yeast, and 1 teaspoon sugar; let stand until foamy.

In a large bowl, combine cottage cheese, eggs, soda, salt, 1/4 cup sugar, margarine, and yeast mixture; mix well. Add green chilies and onions. Stir in enough flour to make dough soft but not sticky. Knead for 8 to 10 minutes. Place dough in a clean, well-greased bowl; cover. Let rise until doubled. Punch down; divide into two balls.

Shape balls into two loaves and place in greased loaf pans; cover. Let rise until doubled. Bake in 350°F oven for 30 to 40 minutes, until tops are brown.

PER SERVING

Calories:	104
Total Fat:	2 g
Cholesterol:	14 mg
Sodium:	257 mg
Carbohydrates:	18 g
Protein:	4 g

Spicy Corn Pudding Bread

Makes 20 servings

1 cup buttermilk
1 cup yellow cornmeal
1 cup unbleached flour
3 teaspoons granulated sugar
1 teaspoon salt
1 teaspoon baking powder
1/2 teaspoon baking soda

1 egg
1/4 cup canola oil
1 8-ounce package frozen whole kernel corn
1 4-ounce can diced green chilies
1 4-ounce jar diced pimientos
2 cups grated cheddar cheese

**A TASTE OF
LATIN AMERICA**

In a large bowl, combine buttermilk and cornmeal. Let stand 30 minutes. Add all remaining ingredients (except cheese) to cornmeal mixture; mix well. Fold in cheese. Pour into greased 9" x 13" baking dish. Bake at 375°F for 30 minutes, until top is golden brown.

PER SERVING

Calories:	142
Total Fat:	7 g
Cholesterol:	23 mg
Sodium:	244 mg
Carbohydrates:	14 g
Protein:	5 g

ITALY

Torte Rustica

JEANNE JARNES

Makes 12 servings

1/3 cup warm water
2 1/2 teaspoons dry yeast
1 teaspoon granulated sugar
2 large eggs
2 tablespoons olive oil
2 cups unbleached flour
1 teaspoon salt
1/2 cup Parmesan cheese, divided
1 10-ounce package frozen spinach,
    thawed and squeezed dry

1 15-ounce container part skim milk ricotta cheese
3/4 cup grated Asiago cheese*, divided
1 cup cut fresh basil
1 egg, beaten
6 slices *Worthington® Frozen Meatless Salami* (optional)
3 ounces part skim milk mozzarella cheese, diced
2 Roma tomatoes*, diced

In a small bowl, combine water, yeast, and sugar; let stand until foamy.

In a large bowl, combine 2 eggs, oil, and yeast mixture; mix well. Add flour, salt, and 1/4 cup Parmesan cheese to liquid mixture. Turn out on smooth surface and knead until smooth, adding flour as needed. Place dough in a greased bowl; cover. Let rise until doubled.

Meanwhile, make filling: In a medium bowl, combine spinach, ricotta, 1/2 cup Asiago cheese, remaining 1/4 cup Parmesan cheese, basil, and half of the beaten egg. Mix well.

*See glossary for definition.

PER SERVING

Calories:	269
Total Fat:	13 g
Cholesterol:	84 mg
Sodium:	539 mg
Carbohydrates:	21 g
Protein:	16 g

Punch down dough; divide in half.

On a floured surface, roll one half into a 14" round. Place on a 13" pizza pan sprayed with nonstick cooking spray (the dough will drape over the edges of the pan.) Place salami on dough, leaving 2" from edge uncovered. Evenly spread ricotta mixture over salami; sprinkle with remaining 1/4 cup Asiago. Sprinkle with mozzarella and tomatoes.

Divide remaining dough into 6 equal pieces. Roll each into a 10" rope. Lay ropes across filling to make a lattice. Fold bottom dough up onto filling and crimp to make a raised edge—similar to a pie edge. Brush lattice and edge of dough with reserved egg. Bake torta in a preheated 400°F oven for 25 to 30 minutes or until well browned. Cool for 10 minutes. Serve slightly warm or at room temperature.

SECTION 3

Salads

Greek Spinach Salad

Makes 8 servings

5 cups fresh spinach, thoroughly washed,
    stems removed (tear leaves in half if you wish)

2 ounces feta cheese*, crumbled

1 small red pepper, sliced

2 green onions, sliced

2 teaspoons olive oil

4 teaspoons lemon juice concentrate

1 teaspoon dried oregano

GREECE

In a large salad bowl, toss spinach, feta cheese, pepper, and onion.

In a small mixing bowl, whisk together olive oil, lemon juice, and oregano. Pour over spinach and toss gently. Serve.

*See glossary for definition.

PER SERVING

Calories:	42
Total Fat:	3 g
Cholesterol:	6 mg
Sodium:	108 mg
Carbohydrates:	3 g
Protein:	2 g

CHINA

Mandarin Spinach Salad

WORTHINGTON™ KITCHENS

Makes 6 servings

1 cup chopped *Loma Linda™ Tender Bits*
1 6-ounce can frozen orange juice concentrate
6 cups fresh spinach, washed thoroughly
1/2 cup chopped celery

1/4 cup chopped green onions
1 11-ounce can mandarin oranges, drained
1/2 cup unsalted cashews
1/2 cup fat-free sweet and sour salad dressing

In a small bowl, combine *Tender Bits* and orange juice. Allow to marinate at least 30 minutes.

In a large bowl, combine spinach, celery, green onion, mandarin oranges, and cashews. Drain *Tender Bits* and add to mixture. Toss gently with sweet and sour dressing.

PER SERVING

Calories:	200
Total Fat:	7 g
Cholesterol:	0 mg
Sodium:	200 mg
Carbohydrates:	31 g
Protein:	9 g

Watercress Salad

Makes 6 servings

4 cups watercress*, washed thoroughly, coarse stems removed
1 cup sour cream**
1 tablespoon vinegar
1/2 teaspoon celery seed
Salt to taste

In a large bowl, place watercress.

In a small bowl, combine sour cream, vinegar, celery seed, and salt to taste; mix well. Pour over watercress; toss until mixed. Serve immediately.

IRELAND

*See glossary for definition.

**Lite Version Substitution: You can substitute plain yogurt or low-fat sour cream if you want to cut down on cholesterol.

PER SERVING

Calories:	85
Total Fat:	8 g
Cholesterol:	17 mg
Sodium:	30 mg
Carbohydrates:	2 g
Protein:	2 g

A TASTE OF THE ORIENT

Chinese Cabbage Salad

Makes 10 servings

3 tablespoons almonds
2 tablespoons sesame seeds
1 small Chinese cabbage*, thinly sliced
4 green onions, chopped
1 package oriental flavor ramen noodles, uncooked

1 packet oriental seasoning (from noodle package)
1/2 cup olive oil
2 tablespoons sugar
3 tablespoons vinegar

Toast almonds and sesame seeds in a 350°F oven until golden. *(Watch them carefully so they don't burn.)* Let cool.

In large bowl, combine cabbage and onions.

In a small bowl, combine seasoning from packet, oil, sugar, and vinegar; stir well.

Just before serving, break Ramen noodles into cabbage, sprinkle almonds and sesame seeds over cabbage and noodles. Add dressing; toss well. Serve immediately.

PER SERVING

Calories:	292
Total Fat:	14 g
Cholesterol:	0 mg
Sodium:	208 mg
Carbohydrates:	16 g
Protein:	5 g

*Chinese cabbage (or Napa cabbage) can be found in the produce section of your grocery store.

Sesame Angel Hair Salad

Makes 8 servings

1/2 cup peanut butter (creamy or crunchy)
1/3 cup water
1/4 cup low sodium soy sauce
2 tablespoons rice vinegar*
2 tablespoons sesame oil*
1/2 teaspoon hot pepper sauce
2 cloves garlic, minced

1/2 pound angel hair pasta, uncooked
1/2 pound fresh snow peas, diagonally sliced
5 cups sliced Chinese cabbage**
1 cucumber, peeled and sliced
3 green onions, sliced
1/4 cup chopped peanuts

**A TASTE OF
THE ORIENT**

In a blender, puree peanut butter, water, soy sauce, vinegar, oil, pepper sauce, and garlic until smooth. Set aside.

In a six-quart saucepan, cook pasta according to package instructions. During the last 2 minutes, add snow peas. Drain; rinse under cold water. Drain well.

In a large bowl, combine pasta and cabbage. Add dressing; toss well.

When ready to serve, top with cucumber slices, green onions, and chopped peanuts. Serve hot or cold.

*Rice vinegar and sesame oil can be found in the Oriental food section of your grocery store.
**See asterisk p. 42.

PER SERVING

Calories:	300
Total Fat:	14 g
Cholesterol:	0 mg
Sodium:	400 mg
Carbohydrates:	36 g
Protein:	12 g

SWEDEN

Swedish Beet Salad

NANCY KYTE

Makes 10 servings

- 2 cups cubed canned beets
- 2 cups diced boiled potatoes
- 1/2 cup finely chopped sweet onion
- 1 cup diced peeled apples
- 1/2 teaspoon salt
- 1/2 cup chopped dill pickles
- 1/2 cup chopped walnuts
- 1 teaspoon granulated sugar
- 1 cup light mayonnaise
- 5 teaspoons lemon juice (fresh or from concentrate)
- 1/2 cup light sour cream

In a large bowl, place beets, potatoes, onion, apples, salt, pickles, and walnuts. Cover and refrigerate overnight.

In a small bowl, mix sugar, mayonnaise, lemon juice, and sour cream. When ready to serve, combine dressing and beet mixture. *This will keep for 3 to 4 days.*

PER SERVING

Calories:	163
Total Fat:	9 g
Cholesterol:	10 mg
Sodium:	365 mg
Carbohydrates:	21 g
Protein:	3 g

Cucumber & Tomato Salad [Raita (RI·tah)]

Makes 10 servings

4 whole cucumbers, diced
3 medium tomatoes, diced
1 small onion, diced
1 16-ounce container low-fat sour cream

In a medium bowl, mix cucumbers, tomatoes, and onion. Add sour cream; stir gently. Refrigerate until ready to serve.

This salad is especially good with a spicy entree such as Curry. It "cools" the spiciness.

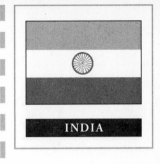

INDIA

PER SERVING

Calories:	62
Total Fat:	1 g
Cholesterol:	4 mg
Sodium:	20 mg
Carbohydrates:	11 g
Protein:	3 g

A TASTE OF THE MIDDLE EAST

Lentil Salad

Makes 8 servings

6 cups water
1 1/2 cups dry lentils
1 teaspoon ground thyme
1 medium onion, quartered
1/8 teaspoon allspice
1/4 cup red wine vinegar

2 teaspoons Dijon mustard
1/2 cup olive oil
2/3 cup chopped celery
2/3 cup shredded carrots
1 cup chopped fresh parsley

In a large saucepan over medium heat, combine water, lentils, thyme, onion, and allspice. Cook 15 to 20 minutes or until lentils are tender. *(Add more water if necessary.)* Discard onion; drain lentils. Rinse with cold water; drain well. Place in a large bowl.

DRESSING: In a medium bowl, mix vinegar, mustard, olive oil, celery, carrots, and parsley. Pour dressing over lentils.

Chill Lentil Salad in refrigerator until cold.

PER SERVING

Calories:	254
Total Fat:	14 g
Cholesterol:	0 mg
Sodium:	35 mg
Carbohydrates:	23 g
Protein:	10 g

Radish Salad

Makes 8 servings

2 bunches radishes, washed and stems removed
1 teaspoon salt
6 tablespoons sour cream
2 teaspoons lemon juice concentrate

Slice radishes thin, but not paper-thin. Place in shallow dish and sprinkle with salt. After 1/2 hour, drain off excess water.

In a serving dish, combine radishes, sour cream, and lemon juice; stir. Serve chilled.

RUSSIA/UKRAINE

PER SERVING

Calories:	26
Total Fat:	2 g
Cholesterol:	5 mg
Sodium:	276 mg
Carbohydrates:	1 g
Protein:	0.4 g

Sesame Chicken Noodle Salad

Makes 8 servings

1 12-ounce package spaghetti, uncooked
1 12.5-ounce can *Worthington® FriChik®*,
    drained and chopped
2 tablespoons sesame oil
2 tablespoons sesame seeds, toasted
3 cloves garlic, chopped
1/2 cup tahini*

1/2 cup broth
    (made with chicken-style broth or seasoning mix)
1 tablespoon sugar
1/3 cup low sodium soy sauce
1/3 cup red wine vinegar
1 bunch scallions, chopped

In a large pot over high heat, bring 2 quarts of water to a boil; cook pasta. When tender, drain. Refill pot with cold water; return pasta to pot. Let stand until completely cool; drain thoroughly.

In a large bowl, combine pasta, *FriChik®*, and 1 tablespoon of sesame oil; mix well. Cover; set aside.

In a shallow baking pan, toast sesame seeds in a 350°F oven until golden brown. Set aside.

In a blender or food processor, process garlic, tahini, broth, sugar, soy sauce, vinegar, and remaining oil for 15 seconds. Add to pasta mixture; mix well. Cover; refrigerate at least 2 hours and up to 2 days.

To serve, turn mixture out onto a large serving platter. Sprinkle sesame seeds over center and scallions around edge.

*See glossary for definition.

PER SERVING

Calories:	354
Total Fat:	15 g
Cholesterol:	0 mg
Sodium:	643 mg
Carbohydrates:	41 g
Protein:	13 g

Toasted Bread Salad [Fatoosh]

Makes 6 servings

3 whole pita bread rounds,
    toasted and torn into bite-sized pieces
1/2 cup chopped fresh mint
1 head iceberg lettuce, cut into bite-sized pieces
1 bunch green onions, sliced
3 medium tomatoes, cut into wedges

1 medium cucumber, peeled and sliced
1/2 cup chopped fresh parsley
1/3 cup olive oil
1/2 cup fresh-squeezed lemon juice
1 clove garlic, diced
Salt to taste

In a large bowl, combine pita, mint, lettuce, onion, tomato, cucumber, and parsley.

In a small bowl, combine oil, lemon juice, garlic, and salt. Pour over bread and vegetables; toss well. Serve immediately.

A TASTE OF THE MIDDLE EAST

PER SERVING

Calories:	278
Total Fat:	13 g
Cholesterol:	0 mg
Sodium:	186 mg
Carbohydrates:	37 g
Protein:	7 g

SWEDEN

Cranberry Salad

NANCY KYTE

Makes 12 servings

16 ounces fresh cranberries, frozen*
1 cup granulated sugar
1 8-ounce can crushed pineapple, drained
8 ounces miniature marshmallows
1 12-ounce container lite (or low-fat) whipped topping, softened

In a food processor, pulse frozen cranberries until chopped.

In a large bowl, combine chopped cranberries and sugar. *This can be refrigerated overnight.* After sugar dissolves, add pineapple and marshmallows; fold in whipped topping.

This is beautiful served in a crystal bowl.

PER SERVING

Calories:	220
Total Fat:	4 g
Cholesterol:	0 mg
Sodium:	31 mg
Carbohydrates:	45 g
Protein:	1 g

*Freezing fresh cranberries will make them easier to chop.

Fruit Salad

Makes 20 servings

1 11-ounce can mandarin oranges, drained
1 16-ounce can fruit cocktail, drained
1 20-ounce can pineapple chunks in juice, drained
2 cups green grapes (halved if large)

3 cups miniature marshmallows
1 1-pound package shredded coconut
1 1/2 cups lowfat sour cream

In a large bowl, combine all ingredients. Mix well; chill.

HAWAII, USA

PER SERVING

Calories:	155
Total Fat:	8 g
Cholesterol:	1 mg
Sodium:	14 mg
Carbohydrates:	21 g
Protein:	2 g

SECTION 4

Entrees

Kabobs

Jacquie Randall

Makes 12 servings

1 16-ounce package frozen *Worthington® Chic-Kettes®*, thawed and torn into large pieces

3 Portobello mushrooms*, sliced into large pieces

1 small onion, chopped

1 8-ounce jar prepared sweet and sour sauce

12 kumquats, halved

12 cherry tomatoes, halved

3 plums, quartered

2 large green peppers, cut into big pieces

2 large red bell peppers, cut into big pieces

12 green onions, cut so about 2" of green remains

1/4 pound asparagus spears

10" skewers**

VEGAN

In a medium skillet (sprayed with nonstick cooking spray) over medium-high heat, sauté *Chic-Kettes®* pieces, mushrooms, and onion. Add sweet and sour sauce; simmer for 3 minutes. Store in a container until ready to assemble kabobs. *(The kumquats and green and red peppers can be prepared ahead of time and stored in the refrigerator.)* Just before assembling kabobs, sauté green onions and asparagus tips in a small amount of oil to soften. Set aside until ready to use.

Assemble by sliding fruit, vegetables, mushrooms, and *Chic-Kettes®* onto skewers in any order you like. Place on large cookie sheets. Sprinkle with salt and bake at 350°F for about 1/2 hour. *Vegetables, fruit, and mushrooms should be tender but firm—not mushy.* Serve hot.

You can also use an outdoor barbecue to grill your kabobs.

*See glossary for definition.
**Skewers can be purchased at most grocery stores or party supply stores.

PER SERVING	
Calories:	190
Total Fat:	6 g
Cholesterol:	0 mg
Sodium:	372 mg
Carbohydrates:	27 g
Protein:	11 g

CHINA

Chinese Spring Rolls

CORINNA CHEANG

Makes 12 servings

4 tablespoons canola oil
4 cloves garlic, chopped
1 medium jícama*, peeled and shredded (about 4 cups)
1/2 of an 8-ounce package *Worthington® Frozen Meatless Smoked Turkey*, sliced into strips
1 large carrot, shredded

Pinch ofsalt
1 tablespoon vegetarian oyster sauce or soy sauce
24 egg roll wrappers

In a large skillet over medium-high heat, sauté garlic in oil for 3 minutes. Add jícama, turkey, carrot, salt, and oyster or soy sauce. Fry until jícama is tender but not mushy.

Place a tablespoon of jícama mixture in the center of each egg roll skin and roll tightly in egg roll fashion (see example). Seal open edges by rubbing with water. *(Otherwise, the filling may leak out during frying.)* Deep fry until crisp and golden. Drain on paper towels.

*See glossary for definition.

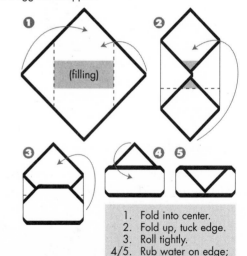

1. Fold into center.
2. Fold up, tuck edge.
3. Roll tightly.
4/5. Rub water on edge; fold over.

PER SERVING

Calories:	127
Total Fat:	5 g
Cholesterol:	1 mg
Sodium:	242 mg
Carbohydrates:	15 g
Protein:	4 g

Vietnamese Spring Rolls

LOC AND HYEN NGUYEN

VIETNAM

Makes 15 servings

12 eggs, well beaten
2 pounds carrots, shredded
2 pounds jícama*, peeled and shredded
4 green onions, shredded
2 pounds mushrooms, sliced

1/2 teaspoon garlic salt
Pinch of sugar
1 package egg roll skins (30 pieces)
Oil for deep-frying
Plum sauce**

In a medium skillet (sprayed with nonstick cooking spray), fry eggs until very dry and in small pieces. Set aside.

In a large skillet (sprayed with nonstick cooking spray) over medium heat, fry carrot, jícama, green onion, and mushrooms until tender. Sprinkle garlic salt and sugar over vegetables. Remove from heat. Add eggs; stir until mixed.

Place 1 tablespoon of vegetable mixture close to one edge of the egg roll skin. Roll up to form egg roll (see instructions p. 54). Fry in hot oil (use candy thermometer to register temperature for deep-frying) until golden brown. Remove and serve immediately with plum sauce.

*See glossary for definition.
**Plum sauce can be found in the international foods section of your grocery store.

PER SERVING

Calories:	142
Total Fat:	2 g
Cholesterol:	1 mg
Sodium:	229 mg
Carbohydrates:	25 g
Protein:	7 g

A TASTE OF AFRICA

African Bean Burritos

CAROL DODGE

Makes 10 burritos

1 tablespoon oil
1/4 cup chopped onion
1 clove garlic, minced
3 tablespoons chunky peanut butter
1 29-ounce can sweet potatoes, drained
1 15-ounce can red beans, drained
1 teaspoon ground cumin

1/2 teaspoon ground cinnamon
1/8 teaspoon cayenne pepper
10 8-inch flour tortillas
3/4 cup salsa
6 tablespoons sour cream
1/4 cup chopped green onions (including green tops)
2 tablespoons chopped cilantro

In large skillet over medium heat, sauté onion (not green onion) and garlic in oil until tender, stirring constantly. Stir in peanut butter, sweet potatoes, and beans; mash slightly. Add cumin, cinnamon, and pepper; mix well. Reduce heat to low and simmer, covered, for 2 to 3 minutes or until thoroughly heated, stirring occasionally.

Meanwhile, heat tortillas. Spread a scant 1/2 cup sweet potato mixture across center of each tortilla. Top each with 2 tablespoons salsa, 1 tablespoon sour cream, 2 teaspoons chopped green onions, and 1 teaspoon cilantro. Spread to cover sweet potato mixture. Fold in burrito fashion. Serve.

The combination of peanut butter and spices adds a whole new twist to this delightful burrito. Don't worry, those of you who are not fond of peanut butter, you really can't single it out. It blends in with the other ingredients.

PER SERVING

Calories:	327
Total Fat:	9 g
Cholesterol:	4 mg
Sodium:	279 mg
Carbohydrates:	53 g
Protein:	10 g

Cornmeal Tarts

PAT GILBERT

Makes 48 tarts

TEX-MEX

2 cups unbleached flour
1 teaspoon salt
1 cup cornmeal
2/3 cup shortening

2/3 cup shredded cheddar cheese
2/3 cup water
1 1/2 cups refried beans

In large bowl, combine flour, salt, and cornmeal. Cut in shortening until mixture resembles coarse crumbs. Stir in cheese. Add water; form into a ball.

Roll out 48 balls; pat into mini muffin tins. Bake in a 400°F oven for 15 minutes or until golden brown. Remove and fill tarts with refried beans. Garnish with an olive, vegetable, or sour cream.

SERVING SUGGESTION: These tarts make great appetizers. Also, you can freeze the tart shells—or filled tarts—for later use.

PER SERVING
Calories:	69
Total Fat:	3 g
Cholesterol:	2 mg
Sodium:	88 mg
Carbohydrates:	8 g
Protein:	2 g

INDIA

VEGAN

PER SERVING

(Samosas with Nimikies)

Calories:	127
Total Fat:	6 g
Cholesterol:	1 mg
Sodium:	221 mg
Carbohydrates:	17 g
Protein:	2 g

Samosas

Makes 10 servings

1 1/2 cups mashed potatoes (from scratch with salt, or from packaged mashed potatoes)
1/2 cup frozen peas and carrots
2 teaspoons curry powder*
2 cloves garlic, minced
1 tablespoon lemon juice (optional)

In a medium bowl, mix mashed potatoes and other ingredients together, stirring well. Put spoonfuls on rolled out Nimkies pastry (see p. 59). Fry in canola heated to 375°F, only until puffy and golden.

SERVING SUGGESTION: Serve hot with a sauce made out of plain yogurt, finely chopped cucumber, chopped chili, and chopped mint. Instead of frying, you can experiment with baking as well. The texture will be different.

DONNA KROGSTAD CONTRIBUTED A QUICK WAY TO MAKE SAMOSAS WITHOUT NIMKIES: Cut 5 medium flour tortillas in half. In each half-circle place a large spoonful of filling. Fold sides over the filling in thirds forming a triangle (see example.) Dab water inside the circular portion of the folded tortilla; pinch the edges tightly to seal. Fry in oil that is heated to 375°F until golden brown, and drain on paper towel.

*You may chose to cut down on the curry powder.

Nimkies

1 cup unbleached flour
1 teaspoon baking powder
1/2 teaspoon salt
1/2 teaspoon cumin

1/4 teaspoon turmeric
1/4 teaspoon chili powder
2 tablespoons shortening
3 1/2 tablespoons cold water

Make Samosa mixture (recipe on preceding page).

In a medium bowl, mix flour, baking powder, salt, cumin, turmeric, and chili powder. Use a pastry blender to cut in shortening until mixture resembles coarse meal. Add enough cold water to make a stiff dough—similar to pastry. Roll out very thin on a floured surface.

See Samosas recipe for further instructions and serving suggestions.

A TASTE OF THE MIDDLE EAST

Mediterranean Pita Rounds

PAT OWENS

Makes 8 servings

2 15-ounce cans garbanzo beans
1/4 cup skim milk
1/4 cup fresh lemon juice
5 cloves garlic, chopped
8 8-inch pita bread rounds
1 teaspoon olive oil
1 10-ounce package frozen chopped spinach,
    thawed and drained

2 cups chopped tomato
1 cup diced green bell pepper
1 cup diced red bell pepper
1/2 cup crumbled feta cheese*
1/3 cup sliced black olives

In a food processor or blender, process garbanzo beans, milk, lemon juice, and garlic until smooth. Set aside.

Arrange pita rounds on an ungreased baking sheet; brush with olive oil. Bake at 450°F for 6 minutes. Remove from oven; spread bean mixture evenly over pitas to 1/2" from edge. Arrange spinach and remaining ingredients evenly over pita rounds. Bake at 450°F for 5 minutes or until thoroughly heated and crust is crisp.

PER SERVING

Calories:	287
Total Fat:	4 g
Cholesterol:	7 mg
Sodium:	660 mg
Carbohydrates:	51 g
Protein:	11 g

*See glossary for definition.

Sfeeha

Makes 10 servings

2 1/2 teaspoons dry yeast
1/2 cup warm water (112°F)
Pinch of sugar
2 1/2 cups unbleached flour
1 teaspoon salt
1/2 cup olive oil

1 cup warm water
1 20-ounce can *Loma Linda® Vege-Burger®*
1 medium onion, chopped
1/2 cup pine nuts*
Juice of one lemon

In a small bowl, dissolve yeast in 1/2 cup warm water and a pinch of sugar. Let stand until foamy.

In a large bowl, measure flour. Add yeast mixture, salt, oil, and remaining 1 cup water. Make into a smooth dough; knead 10 minutes on a smooth surface. Place in a clean, greased bowl; cover with a towel. Let stand until doubled.

In a medium bowl, combine *Vege-Burger®*, onion, pine nuts, and lemon juice.

Divide dough into 10 pieces; flatten with your fingers. Place a tablespoon of filling in center. Fold one side over to meet other edge—like turnovers—or fold edges in, leaving center open. Place Sfeehas on an oiled baking sheet. Bake at 375°F for 15 minutes or until dough is golden.

HELPFUL HINT: Make it simpler on yourself—purchase 2 cans ready-to-bake breadsticks from the refrigerated section of your local grocery and use in place of handmade dough.

*See glossary for definition.

SYRIA

VEGAN

PER SERVING

Calories:	329
Total Fat:	17 g
Cholesterol:	0 mg
Sodium:	331 mg
Carbohydrates:	28 g
Protein:	16 g

A TASTE OF THE MIDDLE EAST

Falafels

NORMA VAIL

Makes 10 servings

1 20-ounce can garbanzo beans
1/3 cup water
1 slice whole-wheat bread
1 tablespoon flour
1/2 teaspoon baking soda
3 cloves garlic, finely chopped
1 egg, slightly beaten
2 tablespoons chopped fresh parsley

3/4 teaspoon salt
1/4 teaspoon ground cumin
1/2 teaspoon turmeric
1/4 teaspoon dried basil
1/4 teaspoon dried marjoram
1 tablespoon canola oil
Oil (for deep-frying)
Flour (to coat)

In a food processor or blender, process garbanzo beans until smooth. Add all other ingredients; process. *Mixture will be soft.*

In a medium saucepan over medium-high heat, heat frying oil* to 365°F. Form falafel mixture into 1" balls. Coat with flour; fry 4 or 5 at a time in hot oil. *The balls rise to the surface and are light brown when cooked (about 2 minutes).* Drain on paper towels.

SERVING SUGGESTION: Serve in pita pocket bread with chopped onion, tomato, and lettuce.

*The oil absorbed during deep-frying is not included in the nutritional analysis.

PER SERVING

Calories:	196
Total Fat:	3 g
Cholesterol:	21 mg
Sodium:	585 mg
Carbohydrates:	35 g
Protein:	7 g

Tofu Patties

SUSAN ROBINSON

JAPAN

Makes 8 servings

16 ounces firm tofu, drained
1 cup fresh bean sprouts
1/2 cup grated carrots
1/2 cup chopped onion

1/2 teaspoon salt
1 teaspoon soy sauce
2 tablespoons sliced green onion
1 egg

Squeeze as much liquid as possible from tofu if water-packed.

In a large bowl, crumble tofu. Add remaining ingredients; mix well.

In a large skillet (sprayed with nonstick cooking spray) over medium-high heat, drop mixture by spoonfuls; flatten to 1/2" thick patties. Brown on both sides.

SERVING SUGGESTION: Serve with soy sauce, catsup, or thin gravy.

PER SERVING

Calories:	64
Total Fat:	3 g
Cholesterol:	27 mg
Sodium:	175 mg
Carbohydrates:	4 g
Protein:	6 g

TEX-MEX

Chiles Relleños [CHEE·lehs rreh·YEH·nohs]

Barbara Mitzelfelt

Makes 6 relleños

6 Anaheim (or long green) chili peppers
1/2 teaspoon salt
2 tablespoons canola oil
1/2 cup unbleached flour
1/2 pound Monterey Jack cheese, cut into 4" x 1" x 1/4" strips
5 eggs, separated

Broil both sides of whole chilies until brown spots and blistering appears on the skins. Cool slightly and peel. *To save time, you could substitute canned whole, roasted chilies.* After peeling, slice an opening down one side of the chili; remove seeds. Fill with a slice of Monterey Jack cheese.

In a medium bowl, beat egg whites until stiff. Add yolks all at once; mix.

In a separate bowl, measure flour. Dip stuffed chilies in flour, then egg mixture. Deep-fry in oil until golden brown on both sides.

PER SERVING

Calories:	305
Total Fat:	20 g
Cholesterol:	213 mg
Sodium:	437 mg
Carbohydrates:	14 g
Protein:	17 g

Ecuadorian Rice Omelet

MELANIE ROMERO

Makes 8 servings

4 cups cooked white or brown rice (if using leftover rice, warm before using)
1 1/4 cups *Morningstar Farms® Scramblers®*
1/2 teaspoon salt
1/2 teaspoon garlic powder
1/2 teaspoon onion powder

In a medium bowl, mix rice, *Scramblers®,* and seasonings.

In a 10" skillet over medium heat, heat oil. Pour egg batter into pan; cook as you would an omelet, until set. Invert a plate over the top of the pan; quickly turn over omelet onto plate. Slide omelet back into skillet, cooking other side until slightly browned. Turn onto plate; cut into 8 wedges. *This is similar to a frittata, except you cook it on both sides on top of the stove.*

SERVING SUGGESTION: Sprinkle with fresh chopped parsley, cilantro, or any dried herb. Sprinkle with grated cheese such as jack, mozzarella, or cheddar. Serve with a favorite salsa. Great for breakfast or brunch.

ECUADOR

PER SERVING

Calories:	154
Total Fat:	2 g
Cholesterol:	0 mg
Sodium:	188 mg
Carbohydrates:	27 g
Protein:	6 g

**A TASTE OF
THE ORIENT**

*Egg foo yong is a Chinese-
American dish.*

Egg Foo Yong With Chicken

Makes 8 servings

1 12.5-ounce can *Worthington® FriChik®*, diced
1 1/2 cups fresh bean sprouts
1/3 cup sliced green onion
Salt to taste
5 eggs or 1 1/4 cups *Morningstar Farms® Scramblers®**

1 tablespoon canola oil
2 cups vegetable broth
2 tablespoons cornstarch
2 tablespoons low-sodium soy sauce
Salt to taste

In a large bowl, combine *FriChik®,* bean sprouts, green onion, and salt.

In a medium bowl, beat eggs. Add at once to sprout mixture; stir.

In a large skillet over medium heat, fry 1/4 cup of bean sprout mixture in oil until brown; turn to brown other side.

HOT SOY SAUCE: In a medium saucepan over medium-high heat, heat broth. In small bowl, mix cornstarch and soy sauce. Pour 1/2 cup hot broth into cornstarch mixture; stir till lumps are gone. Pour cornstarch mixture into saucepan of vegetable broth; stir until thickened. Serve with Egg Foo Yong.

PER SERVING

Calories:	129
Total Fat:	5 g
Cholesterol:	1 mg*
Sodium:	765 mg
Carbohydrates:	11 g
Protein:	9 g

*What a vast difference in cholesterol between whole eggs and *Scramblers®!*
Cholesterol: 1 mg (*Scramblers®*) verses 162 mg (whole eggs)

Enchiladas

KARIN GORTON

Makes 15 servings

TEX-MEX

1 19-ounce can medium enchilada sauce	1 teaspoon ground cumin
1 19-ounce can mild enchilada sauce	1 teaspoon mexican seasoning
1 16-ounce can black olives, drained and sliced	1/2 pound cheddar cheese, grated
1 30-ounce can meatless chili beans, drained	1/2 pound Monterey Jack cheese, grated
1/2 teaspoon paprika	21 corn tortillas

In a large bowl, mix the enchilada sauces, olives, chili beans, and seasonings.

In a separate bowl, combine grated cheeses.

Spray 9" x 13" glass baking dish with nonstick cooking spray. Spread a small amount of the enchilada sauce mixture in the bottom of the pan. Arrange 7 tortillas on the enchilada sauce. *Tear some of the tortillas to fit in the pan if necessary.* Layer with enchilada sauce mixture and grated cheeses. Repeat layers ending with sauce and cheese. Bake at 350°F for 40 to 50 minutes.

PER SERVING

Calories:	351
Total Fat:	20 g
Cholesterol:	49 mg
Sodium:	763 mg
Carbohydrates:	30 g
Protein:	14 g

RUSSIA

Stuffed Cabbage Leaves [Hulabshi (huh·LAB·shee)]

Makes 12 servings

1 tablespoon margarine	1/2 cup vegetable stock
1/3 cup shredded carrots	12 green cabbage leaves
2 tablespoons chopped onion	1 20-ounce can *Loma Linda® Vege-Burger®*
2 cups chopped fresh tomatoes	1 egg
1/4 teaspoon salt	1/2 cup chopped onion
1/8 teaspoon ground allspice	1 cup cooked barley or rice
1/4 cup unbleached flour	1 teaspoon salt
1/4 cup water	2 tablespoons canola oil

SAUCE: In small skillet, sauté carrot and 2 tablespoons onion in margarine for 3 minutes. Add tomatoes, 1/4 teaspoon salt, and allspice. Cover and simmer until carrot is tender. In a small bowl, combine flour and water. Mix into a smooth paste—there should be no lumps. Pour vegetable stock into flour paste; add to carrot mixture. Heat to boiling and cook until thickened.

In a large saucepan over high heat, cook cabbage leaves in salted water for 5 minutes. Drain.

In a medium bowl, combine burger, egg, 1/2 cup onion, barley or rice, and salt.

In a medium skillet over medium-high heat, brown burger mixture in oil. Place one spoonful of burger mixture on each steamed cabbage leaf. Fold edges in and roll up. *(Fasten with a toothpick if you choose.)*

In a 9" x 13" baking dish, pour sauce. Place cabbage rolls in sauce; cover with foil. Bake in a 350°F oven for 45 minutes.

PER SERVING

Calories:	138
Total Fat:	5 g
Cholesterol:	18 mg
Sodium:	411 mg
Carbohydrates:	11 g
Protein:	11 g

Veranike (veh·RA·nuh·kee)

SHARON LEWIS

Makes 16 servings

2 3/4 cups unbleached flour
2 eggs
1 teaspoon salt
1 teaspoon sugar
2/3 cup cold water

2 cups dry curd cottage cheese
2 eggs
Salt to taste
1 pint whipping cream*

RUSSIA/UKRAINE

In a large mixing bowl, combine flour, eggs, salt, sugar, and water. Mix well; turn out onto a smooth surface. Knead for 30 seconds. *It should be satiny smooth.*

In a 2-quart kettle, bring 6 cups water to a soft, rolling boil.

On a clean, floured surface, use a rolling pin to roll dough until thin. Cut with a large biscuit cutter or mouth of a glass. Place 1 tablespoon of cottage cheese mixture in center of stamped dough, fold dough; pinch the edges to seal. Drop veranikes into boiling water; cook for 4 minutes. Drain; place in 9" x 13" baking dish.

Pour unwhipped whipping cream over Veranikes. Bake at 350°F for 20 to 30 minutes. Serve hot.

VARIATION: Omit whipping cream and bake, covered, for 20 minutes. Serve with a dollop of sour cream or plain, non-fat yogurt.

*Whipping cream nutritional information has not been calculated.

PER SERVING

Calories:	113
Total Fat:	2 g
Cholesterol:	55 mg
Sodium:	152 mg
Carbohydrates:	17 g
Protein:	7 g

MEXICO

Chicken Casserole Mexicali

BETTY BROOKS

Makes 15 servings

2 12.5-ounce cans *Worthington® FriChik®*, drained
1 medium onion, chopped
Pinch of cayenne pepper
Pinch of chili powder
Pinch of garlic powder
1 pound processed American cheese, grated

1 10-ounce can tomatoes with green chilies
1 10.75-ounce can condensed cream of mushroom
    soup, undiluted
1 10.75-ounce can condensed cream of celery soup,
    undiluted
1 10.5-ounce package corn chips

Cut *FriChik®* pieces in half and arrange in a 9" x 13" baking dish. Sprinkle chopped onion and seasonings on top. Cover with grated cheese.

In a medium bowl, mix canned tomatoes with both cans of soup; spoon over the cheese layer. Lightly crush the corn chips; sprinkle on top of the soup layer. Bake at 375°F 30 to 40 minutes, or until bubbly and cheese is melted.

SERVING SUGGESTION: Good with rice, noodles, or just by itself.

PER SERVING

Calories:	301
Total Fat:	21 g
Cholesterol:	29 mg
Sodium:	1009 mg
Carbohydrates:	16 g
Protein:	12 g

Chicken Kiev

MARY SCHWANTES

Makes 10 servings

1/4 cup butter
1/4 cup unbleached flour
1 1/2 cups vegetable broth
1/8 teaspoon ground nutmeg
1/2 cup whipping cream, whipped

1 cup grated Parmesan cheese
1 1/2 pounds fresh broccoli flowerets,
    cooked and drained
1 12.5-ounce can *Worthington® FriChik®*,
    drained and sliced

UKRAINE

SAUCE: In a medium saucepan over medium-high heat, melt butter; blend in flour. Cook, stirring constantly, until mixture has thickened and is smooth. Remove from heat; stir in vegetable broth. Return to heat; bring to a boil. Boil for one minute, stirring constantly. Remove from heat; stir in nutmeg. Gently fold in whipped cream and 1/2 cup Parmesan cheese.

After cooking broccoli, place in an ungreased casserole dish. Top with *FriChik®* slices. Pour sauce over *FriChik®* and sprinkle with remaining 1/2 cup Parmesan cheese. If serving immediately, set oven to broil until cheese is golden. If you will be serving this the next day, refrigerate. When ready to serve, place uncovered in a 350°F oven for 35 to 45 minutes, until heated through.

PER SERVING

Calories:	203
Total Fat:	14 g
Cholesterol:	35 mg
Sodium:	567 mg
Carbohydrates:	11 g
Protein:	9 g

FRANCE

Chicken Morengo

Makes 6 servings

1 12.5-ounce can *Worthington® FriChik®*, quartered
1/2 teaspoon salt
1 teaspoon paprika
3 tablespoons margarine
1/4 cup chopped onion
1/2 cup vegetable broth

1 cup fresh sliced mushrooms
1 10.75-ounce can condensed cream of mushroom
   soup, undiluted
1/8 teaspoon hot sauce
1/4 cup currant jelly*

In a bowl, sprinkle *FriChik®* with salt and paprika.

In a large skillet over medium-high heat, melt 2 tablespoons margarine. Brown *FriChik®;* add onion and vegetable broth. Bring to a boil. Reduce heat; simmer.

In a medium skillet over medium heat, use remaining 1 tablespoon margarine to sauté mushrooms for 2 minutes. Add mushroom soup, hot sauce, and currant jelly; stir until mixed. Pour over *FriChik®* and heat through. Serve hot.

PER SERVING

Calories:	207
Total Fat:	13 g
Cholesterol:	1 mg
Sodium:	976 mg
Carbohydrates:	17 g
Protein:	6 g

*If currant jelly is not available at your local supermarket, try a gourmet or specialty store.

Corn Tortilla Casserole

LOIDA MORALES

Makes 15 servings

24 corn tortillas, cut into 1" pieces
1 10.75-ounce can condensed cream of celery soup, undiluted
1 10.75-ounce can condensed cream of mushroom soup, undiluted
1/2 soup can of milk

2 4-ounce cans diced green chilies
1 cup chopped onion
2 tablespoons margarine, melted
2 cups shredded Monterey Jack cheese
Salt to taste

MEXICO

In a small skillet over medium-high heat, sauté onion in 2 tablespoons margarine until tender.

In a large bowl, mix soups, milk, and chilies. Add corn tortilla pieces and sautéed onion; stir well.

Pour half of tortilla mixture into 9" x 13" baking dish. Sprinkle 1/2 of the cheese over mixture. Repeat layers; top with cheese. Bake at 350°F for 40 to 50 minutes.

PER SERVING
Calories: 192
Total Fat: 9 g
Cholesterol: 16 mg
Sodium: 366 mg
Carbohydrates: 22 g
Protein: 7 g

A TASTE OF THE ORIENT

Hong Kong Casserole

Makes 8 servings

1/2 of a 20-ounce can *Worthington® Multigrain Cutlets®*, sliced into strips

1 10.75-ounce can condensed cream of mushroom soup, undiluted

3/4 cup evaporated milk

1 4-ounce can sliced mushrooms, drained

8 ounces frozen peas

1 cup diced celery

1 8 1/2-ounce can chow mein noodles

1/4 cup chopped onion

1/2 cup cashews

In a large bowl, mix all ingredients, reserving 3/4 cup noodles. Pour into a greased casserole; top with reserved noodles. Bake at 350°F for 45 minutes.

PER SERVING

Calories:	308
Total Fat:	17 g
Cholesterol:	7 mg
Sodium:	431 mg
Carbohydrates:	30 g
Protein:	11 g

Manicotti

Makes 10 servings

- 1 8-ounce package manicotti pasta
- 16 ounces firm tofu, crumbled
- 1/2 cup soybean mayonnaise*
- 1/4 cup soy milk
- 1 teaspoon onion powder
- 1/2 teaspoon garlic powder
- 1/2 teaspoon salt
- 1 26-ounce can spaghetti sauce

ITALY

VEGAN

Cook manicotti according to package instructions. Drain; set aside.

In a medium bowl, mash tofu. Add all other ingredients except pasta and sauce; stir well. Stuff manicotti with tofu mixture. Place in 9" x 13" baking dish. Pour spaghetti sauce over shells. Bake at 350°F for 30 to 40 minutes. Serve topped with grated soy cheese if desired.

The filling is such a close second to cottage cheese, you will love it!

*TO MAKE YOUR OWN SOYBEAN MAYONNAISE, HERE IS THE RECIPE:
- 1 cup water
- 1 teaspoon salt
- 3/4 rounded dehydrated soy milk powder
- 1/3 cup oil
- 1/4 cup lemon juice

In a blender, process water, salt, soy milk powder, and oil until smooth. Slowly add 1/4 cup lemon juice. *Recipe courtesy of Blanche Fisher.*

PER SERVING	
Calories:	300
Total Fat:	14 g
Cholesterol:	0 mg
Sodium:	491 mg
Carbohydrates:	31 g
Protein:	12 g

INDIA

VEGAN

Indian Nut Loaf

JAYMEE FRIMML

Makes 20 servings

3 tablespoons canola oil
2 cups finely shredded cabbage
2 cups finely diced celery
2 cups finely chopped green peppers
1 teaspoon asafetida (see p. 77)
1/2 cup finely ground cashews
1/2 cup finely ground walnuts
1/2 cup finely ground almonds
1 cup cooked brown rice
1 cup slightly ground regular oats

1/2 teaspoon salt
1/2 teaspoon cayenne pepper
1/2 teaspoon ground thyme
1/2 teaspoon basil
2 teaspoons ground sage
4 packages chicken-like broth or seasoning mix
1 1/2 cups tomato puree
2 cups firm tofu
Spaghetti sauce

In a medium skillet over medium-high heat, sauté cabbage, celery, peppers, and asafetida in 2 tablespoons of oil until tender. Remove from heat.

In a large bowl, combine sautéed vegetables with nuts and other ingredients (except spaghetti sauce). Mix with a spoon—or by hand to get a better feel for things. If mixture is too wet, add more oats; if too dry add spaghetti sauce. It should be a thick mixture that can be scooped and packed into two well-greased loaf pans or one 7" x 11" baking dish. Bake at 350°F for 45 to 60 minutes. Let stand for 20 minutes before serving.

To serve, cut into 15 pieces. Place each piece on a fresh cabbage leaf, spoon spaghetti sauce over it and sprinkle with slivered almonds. Serve with steamed baby carrots and green peas or a fresh green salad.

PER SERVING

Calories:	168
Total Fat:	10 g
Cholesterol:	0 mg
Sodium:	209 mg
Carbohydrates:	13 g
Protein:	8 g

Asafetida
[ah-sah-FEH-teh-dah]

Asafetida is a spice used in India and the Middle East that belongs to the parsley family. The milk from the root is obtained and dried, and usually mixed with rice flour to make it less pungent and easier to add to foods. It has a bitter taste by itself, and a very pungent unpleasant smell. It is used in very small quantities. After cooking in food it gives a very rich pleasant taste. It can be obtained in any Indian or Pakistani shop. Keep in an airtight container as the odor can easily permeate into other foods. It can last up to 10 years but the smell becomes less pungent.

The Indian Nut Loaf recipe has been added as a "teaser" to those who are really adventurous.

GREECE

"Nine Bean Loaf®" With Yogurt Sauce

WORTHINGTON™ KITCHENS

Makes 6 servings

1 15-ounce package *Natural Touch® Nine Bean Loaf®*
8 ounces plain lowfat yogurt
2 ounces crumbled feta cheese*
1/4 cup diced onion
1/2 teaspoon garlic powder
1/2 teaspoon dried basil

Prepare *Nine Bean Loaf®* according to package instructions.

SAUCE: In a small bowl, combine yogurt and remaining ingredients. Refrigerate until time to serve. Pour sauce over each serving of *Nine Bean Loaf®*.

PER SERVING

Calories:	200
Total Fat:	1 g
Cholesterol:	0 mg
Sodium:	480 mg
Carbohydrates:	18 g
Protein:	11 g

*See glossary for definition.

Spinach Pie [Spanakopita (span·uh·KOH·pih·tuh)]

Makes 15 servings

2 tablespoons canola oil
1 medium onion, chopped
1 10-ounce package frozen spinach, thawed
1 12-ounce container lowfat cottage cheese
1 8-ounce package fat-free cream cheese, softened

1/2 cup crumbled feta cheese*
1/2 teaspoon dried dill weed
1 egg
1 16-ounce package frozen phyllo* dough, thawed
1/2 cup margarine, melted

GREECE

In a large skillet over medium-high heat, sauté onion in canola oil. Drain thawed spinach; squeeze until dry. Add to the onion mixture along with cottage cheese, cream cheese, feta cheese, dill, and egg; mix well.

Remove half of phyllo sheets from package *(keep remaining sheets covered with plastic wrap to prevent drying out)*. Brush bottom and sides of a 9" x 13" baking dish with melted margarine. Place 2 sheets of phyllo in baking dish, pressing phyllo against sides of dish. Brush phyllo with melted margarine; top with 2 more sheets and brush with margarine. Repeat layering and brushing until first half of phyllo is used.

Preheat oven to 350°F. Spread spinach mixture evenly over phyllo sheets in dish. Unwrap remaining phyllo. Place 2 sheets over spinach mixture, letting edges hang over sides of dish; brush with margarine. Repeat layering with remaining phyllo and margarine. Roll edges of phyllo that are hanging over dish inward to form a border. Bake 45 minutes or until crust is golden brown. Remove from oven and let stand for 10 minutes. Garnish with green onions. *This can be used as a main dish or side dish.*

*See glossary for definition.

PER SERVING

Calories:	218
Total Fat:	11 g
Cholesterol:	21 mg
Sodium:	466 mg
Carbohydrates:	19 g
Protein:	9 g

ITALY

Sausage & Tortellini Pasta

Makes 12 servings

16 ounces cheese-filled tortellini
4 cups broccoli flowerets
2 tablespoons margarine
2 tablespoons flour
1 1/2 cups 1% milk

2 cups grated Swiss cheese
2 tablespoons brown mustard
1 8-ounce package *Morningstar Farms®*
    Breakfast Patties, thawed and crumbled

In a large saucepan over medium-high heat, cook tortellini in water according to package directions. After water comes to a boil, reduce heat to simmer. Add broccoli to water; again bring to a boil. Reduce heat; simmer uncovered 5 to 10 minutes, or until tortellini is tender but slightly firm. Stir occasionally. Drain; set aside.

In a medium saucepan, melt margarine; stir in flour. Add milk; stir. Cook over medium-high heat until thickened, *make sure it does not scorch.* Stir in cheese, mustard, and crumbled breakfast patties; cook until cheese melts. Remove from heat.

In a large bowl, combine sausage sauce and drained tortellini; toss well, thoroughly coating the tortellini. Serve hot.

So good!

PER SERVING

Calories:	252
Total Fat:	11 g
Cholesterol:	44 mg
Sodium:	408 mg
Carbohydrates:	20 g
Protein:	17 g

Tagliatelle* With Tomato-Walnut Sauce

Makes 6 servings

2 tablespoons olive oil
1 medium onion, finely chopped
1 stick celery, finely chopped
4 medium tomatoes, chopped
1 medium carrot, grated
2 tablespoons chopped fresh parsley

1 teaspoon red-wine vinegar
1/4 cup water
Salt to taste
3/4 cup chopped walnuts
1 pound fettuccine noodles
4 tablespoons grated Parmesan cheese, optional

ITALY

SAUCE: In a large saucepan over medium heat, sauté onion and celery in 1 tablespoon oil, stirring constantly, for 5 minutes. Add tomatoes, carrot, parsley, vinegar, and water. Reduce heat; simmer for 25 minutes. Season with salt.

In a small skillet over medium-high heat, brown walnuts in remaining 1 tablespoon of oil. Remove from heat.

In a large kettle, boil water; add pasta. Cook just until tender. Drain; return to pan. Add sauce; toss. Serve pasta and sauce topped with walnuts and sprinkled with Parmesan cheese (optional).

PER SERVING

Calories:	351
Total Fat:	12 g
Cholesterol:	2 mg
Sodium:	65 mg
Carbohydrates:	50 g
Protein:	12 g

*"Tagliatelle" (tah·lyuh·TEHL·ee) is the name used in northern Italy for "fettuccine."

JAPAN

Lemon-Apricot Chicken

DOLLY WEBER

Makes 10 servings

1/3 cup margarine, melted
1 egg
2 tablespoons water
1 cup biscuit mix
1 tablespoon lemon zest*
1/4 teaspoon garlic powder

2 12.5-ounce cans *Worthington® FriChik®*, drained
2/3 cup apricot preserves
2 tablespoons lemon juice concentrate
1/2 teaspoon soy sauce
1/4 teaspoon ground ginger

Pour melted margarine into a 9" x 13" baking dish; set aside.

In a medium bowl, beat egg and water until frothy; set aside.

In a medium bowl, combine biscuit mix, lemon zest, and garlic powder; set aside.

Slice each *FriChik®* piece in half lengthwise. Dip each piece into egg mixture, then into biscuit mixture, coating each side. Place in baking dish with melted margarine. Bake in a 425°F oven, uncovered, for 15 minutes. Turn *FriChik®* pieces and bake 10 minutes longer.

In a small bowl, combine apricot preserves, lemon juice, soy sauce, and ginger; mix well. When *FriChik®* has finished baking, pour lemon-apricot sauce over *FriChik®;* return to oven for 10 more minutes. Serve hot.

When I serve this dish, people always ask for the recipe.

*See glossary for definition.

PER SERVING

Calories:	222
Total Fat:	12 g
Cholesterol:	21 mg
Sodium:	459 mg
Carbohydrates:	22 g
Protein:	7 g

Pineapple Sweet & Sour Skallops® I

Dorothy M. Decker

A TASTE OF
THE ORIENT

Makes 8 servings

1 cup flour
2 eggs
4 teaspoons ketchup
6 tablespoons water
1 teaspoon salt
1 20-ounce can *Worthington® Vegetable Skallops®*, drained
1 cup unsweetened pineapple juice
1 cup water

1/4 cup ketchup
1 tablespoon rice vinegar
6 tablespoons sugar
1/4 cup cornstarch
1 tablespoon canola oil
2 medium green peppers
1 medium onion
1 20-ounce can pineapple chunks in syrup, drained

BATTER: In a medium bowl, combine flour, eggs, 4 teaspoons ketchup, 6 tablespoons water, and 1/2 teaspoon salt; beat until mixed well.

In a large skillet, heat enough oil to 350°F for deep-frying*, using a thermometer to test when oil is ready. Dip *Skallops®* into batter, making sure each piece is well coated. Deep-fry pieces until golden brown; drain on paper towels. Arrange on a large platter; set aside.

SAUCE: In a medium bowl, combine pineapple juice with remaining 1 cup water, 1/4 cup ketchup, 1/2 teaspoon salt, vinegar, sugar, and cornstarch; set aside.

In a large skillet over medium-high heat, sauté onion and peppers in 1 tablespoon of oil until crispy-tender. Add sauce mixture to vegetables; cook until bubbly, stirring constantly. Add pineapple chunks; heat through. Pour sauce over deep-fried *Skallops®;* serve.

*The oil absorbed during deep-frying is not included in the nutritional analysis.

PER SERVING	
Calories:	282
Total Fat:	4 g
Cholesterol:	54 mg
Sodium:	610 mg
Carbohydrates:	51 g
Protein:	11 g

Pineapple Sweet & Sour Skallops® II

LORETTA SLACK

Makes 8 servings

1 egg, beaten	1 cup ketchup
1/2 cup unbleached flour	1 tablespoon lemon juice concentrate
1/2 teaspoon garlic powder	1 tablespoon low sodium soy sauce
4 tablespoons canola oil	1/2 cup granulated sugar
1 20-ounce can *Worthington® Vegetable Skallops®*	1 8-ounce can pineapple chunks in juice, drained— reserve liquid
1 medium onion, chopped	1 1/2 tablespoons cornstarch
1 medium green bell pepper, chopped fine	

In a small bowl, combine flour and garlic powder. Dip each *Skallop®* piece in egg then seasoned flour, covering well.

In a large skillet over medium-high heat, fry *Skallops®* in 3 tablespoons of oil until golden brown. Remove from pan; set aside.

In a large skillet over medium-high heat, sauté onion and green pepper in remaining 1 tablespoon of oil until tender. Add ketchup, lemon juice, soy sauce, and sugar; heat through.

Add enough water to pineapple juice to make 1 cup. Add cornstarch to make a paste; stir until lumps dissolve. Add to sautéed vegetable mixture; cook 2 to 3 minutes, stirring constantly, until clear and thickened. Add pineapple chunks; stir well. Add fried *Skallops®* to sauce mixture; mix to coat *Skallops®*. Serve over rice or Chinese noodles.

PER SERVING

Calories:	226
Total Fat:	5 g
Cholesterol:	27 mg
Sodium:	646 mg
Carbohydrates:	36 g
Protein:	10 g

Teriyaki Tofu

Makes 8 servings

1/2 cup low-sodium soy sauce
2 teaspoons honey
2 teaspoons minced fresh gingerroot
2 cloves garlic, minced
2 tablespoons vinegar

1 medium onion, minced
2 pounds extra firm tofu, sliced into 1/2" slices
1/2 cup unbleached flour
1/4 teaspoon salt
2 tablespoons canola oil

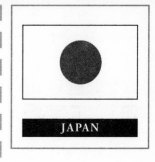

JAPAN

VEGAN

MARINADE: In a small bowl, combine soy sauce, honey, ginger, garlic, vinegar, and onion.

In a shallow baking dish, place sliced tofu; pour on marinade. Let stand for 2 hours. Drain; reserve marinade.

In a medium bowl, mix flour and salt. Dip marinated tofu into flour mixture, coating both sides.

In a large skillet over medium-high heat, heat a small amount of oil. Place flour-coated tofu in hot oil; brown both sides. When all pieces are fried, reduce heat; pour reserved marinade over tofu. Simmer for 10 minutes; serve over rice.

PER SERVING

Calories:	247
Total Fat:	13 g
Cholesterol:	0 mg
Sodium:	683 mg
Carbohydrates:	16 g
Protein:	20 g

INDIA

Curry

SHEILA FANWAR

Makes 8 servings

4 tablespoons canola oil
4 cloves garlic, chopped
3 tablespoons chopped, peeled fresh gingerroot
1 large onion, chopped
2 tablespoons curry powder
2 vegetable bouillon cubes*
2 cups water

2 medium tomatoes, chopped
4 teaspoons tomato sauce
1 8-ounce can unsweetened coconut milk**
4 medium potatoes, cubed
4 ounces frozen green peas
4 tablespoons chopped fresh cilantro

In a large saucepan over medium-high heat, sauté onion in oil until tender. Add garlic and ginger; sauté for 2 more minutes. Add curry powder; cook 2 minutes. Add tomatoes to curry paste; heat back to "bubbling" stage. Cook for 2 minutes. Add bouillon cubes, water, tomato sauce, and coconut milk. Add potatoes and peas; cook at a slow boil until potatoes are tender. Just before serving, add cilantro. Serve over rice.

PER SERVING

Calories:	285
Total Fat:	17 g
Cholesterol:	0 mg
Sodium:	231 mg
Carbohydrates:	30 g
Protein:	5 g

*You will find bouillon cubes in the soup section of your grocery store.
**Lite Version Substitution: use light coconut milk

Garbanzo Curry

Oscar Ramirez

Makes 12 servings

2 tablespoons canola oil
1 1/2 tablespoons chopped fresh ginger
3 cloves garlic, chopped
1 large onion, chopped
1 tablespoon curry powder*
1/2 teaspoon cumin powder
1/2 teaspoon turmeric
1 4-ounce jar chopped pimento

1/2 medium green pepper, chopped
3 stalks celery, diced
1/2 tablespoon chicken-like broth or seasoning mix
1 tablespoon beef-like broth or seasoning mix
1/2 cup tomato puree
2 15.5-ounce cans garbanzo beans, drained—
    reserve liquid
2 tablespoons cornstarch

INDIA

VEGAN

In a large skillet over medium-high heat, sauté ginger, garlic, and onion in oil for 3 minutes. Add curry powder, cumin powder, and turmeric; cook for 2 minutes. Add pimento, green pepper, and celery; cook for 4 more minutes. Add chicken and beef seasonings and tomato puree; cook for 2 minutes. Add garbanzos.

In a medium bowl, add 2 tablespoons cornstarch to reserved garbanzo liquid, stirring until lumps dissolve. Add to garbanzo mixture, stirring until thickened. *If you prefer it a little thicker, add more cornstarch to a small amount of water and pour into mixture.* Serve over rice.

*If you prefer a spicier taste, add more curry powder.

PER SERVING

Calories:	134
Total Fat:	3 g
Cholesterol:	0 mg
Sodium:	501 mg
Carbohydrates:	22 g
Protein:	4 g

THAILAND

VEGAN

Thai Tofu Curry

DANA POTTLE

Makes 8 servings

14 ounces firm tofu cubed

1/4 cup soy sauce

1 medium onion, sliced

4 cloves garlic, sliced

Zest* of one lime or lemon

Juice of one lime or lemon

3 inches fresh gingerroot, sliced

4 teaspoons cumin powder

6 tablespoons chopped fresh cilantro

2 tablespoons soy sauce

2 teaspoons sugar

1 2/3 cups coconut milk**

2 tablespoons peanut oil†

In a baking dish, toss tofu cubes in soy sauce; marinate for 15 minutes.

SAUCE: Meanwhile, in a blender, process all ingredients except tofu and oil until smooth.

In a large skillet over medium-high heat, fry tofu in oil until well browned. Add sauce to tofu and heat through. Serve over jasmine rice.

VARIATION: Sauté sliced fresh mushrooms with the tofu before adding the sauce. Just before serving, spoon the jasmine rice into a large bowl, top with steamed fresh, broccoli flowerets, and spoon the fragrant sauce on top.

This is full of absolutely wonderful flavors. Look out, you might get addicted.

*See glossary for definition.
**Lite Version Substitution: Use light coconut milk.
†If you don't have peanut oil, any type of oil will do.

PER SERVING

Calories:	264
Total Fat:	20 g
Cholesterol:	0 mg
Sodium:	792 mg
Carbohydrates:	15 g
Protein:	11 g

Spicy Vegetable Dahl

Makes 8 servings

1 cup uncooked red or yellow lentils,
    washed and drained
1 teaspoon chopped fresh ginger
1 clove garlic, minced
1 small red chili, seeded and chopped,
    or 1/2 teaspoon chili powder
1 stick celery, chopped
2 tablespoons chopped fresh cilantro
1 tablespoon lemon juice concentrate

5 cups water
3 green onions, sliced
1 medium carrot, chopped
1 tablespoon canola oil
1/2 teaspoon curry powder*
1/4 teaspoon turmeric
1/4 teaspoon ground coriander
1 teaspoon cumin seed
Salt to taste

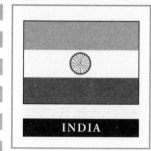

INDIA

In a medium saucepan, combine lentils, ginger, garlic, chili (or chili powder), celery, cilantro, lemon juice, water, green onion, and carrot. Bring to a boil over medium heat, stirring occasionally. Reduce heat; simmer for about 40 minutes or lentils are soft. Transfer to a blender, process until smooth. Return to saucepan; simmer for 5 to 8 minutes, until thickened.

Meanwhile, in a small skillet over medium heat, stir curry powder, turmeric, coriander, and cumin seed in oil until cumin seeds pop. Remove from heat; add to lentil mixture.

SERVING SUGGESTION: Serve dahl over rice with a bit of lemon juice squeezed on top, or dip Chapatis (see p. 27) into it.

*You may want to add more curry powder if Dahl is not spicy enough.

PER SERVING

Calories:	128
Total Fat:	2 g
Cholesterol:	0 mg
Sodium:	25 mg
Carbohydrates:	21 g
Protein:	8 g

A CAJUN FLAVOR

Tofu Etouffee (ay·too·FAY) [Spicy Stew]

CLABERT MENARD

Makes 6 servings

1 pound firm tofu, cut into 1/2" cubes
Cajun spice* to taste
2 tablespoons margarine
1 small green pepper, finely chopped

1 small onion, chopped
1 bunch green onions, chopped
1 24-ounce can crushed tomatoes
Salt to taste

In a small bowl, sprinkle tofu with Cajun spice.

In a large skillet over medium-high heat, brown seasoned tofu in margarine. Remove from skillet with a slotted spoon and set aside. Add green pepper and all onions to skillet; cook until tender. Add tomatoes and tofu; stir gently. If needed, add water to give it a sauce-like consistency. Serve over rice.

PER SERVING

Calories:	253
Total Fat:	11 g
Cholesterol:	0 mg
Sodium:	421 mg
Carbohydrates:	29 g
Protein:	17 g

*Cajun spice is very concentrated, so begin with a conservative amount.

Chik Fried Rice

WORTHINGTON™ KITCHENS

Makes 6 servings

4 ounces *Morningstar Farms® Scramblers®*
1 tablespoon canola oil
1/2 cup chopped green onions
1 cup frozen peas and carrots

4 cups cooked brown rice
1 12.5-ounce can *Worthington® Diced Chik®*, drained
1 tablespoon soy sauce
1/4 teaspoon garlic powder

In a small skillet over low heat, cook *Scramblers®;* chop with spatula. Set aside.

In a large skillet or wok over high heat, stir-fry vegetables in oil for 2 to 3 minutes. Add rice, *Diced Chik®*, soy sauce, and garlic powder; add *Scramblers®*. Continue to stir-fry for 5 more minutes, until rice begins to turn golden brown. *You may need to reduce the heat.*

PER SERVING

Calories:	320
Total Fat:	6 g
Cholesterol:	1 mg
Sodium:	390 mg
Carbohydrates:	54 g
Protein:	11 g

A TASTE OF LATIN AMERICA

VEGAN

Spanish Rice I

Makes 8 servings

2 tablespoons canola oil
1/4 cup chopped onion
2 cloves garlic, diced
1/2 cup diced celery
1/2 cup chopped green bell pepper
1 8-ounce can tomato sauce
1 tablespoon chicken-like broth or seasoning mix

1/8 teaspoon cumin powder
Salt to taste
4 cups cooked rice (use while still warm)
1/4 cup grated carrots
2 cups frozen green peas
2 cups frozen corn

In a large skillet over medium-high heat, sauté onion, garlic, celery, and bell pepper in oil until tender. Add tomato sauce, seasonings, and rice to sauce mixture; add carrots, peas, and corn. When mixture comes to a boil, reduce heat; simmer until moisture is completely absorbed into the rice. Serve hot.

PER SERVING

Calories:	236
Total Fat:	4 g
Cholesterol:	0 mg
Sodium:	467 mg
Carbohydrates:	44 g
Protein:	7 g

Spanish Rice II

Makes 12 servings

1/4 cup canola oil
3 cups uncooked rice
2 cloves garlic, chopped
1 small onion, chopped
6 cups water

1 cup frozen mixed vegetables
3 *Loma Linda® Linkettes®*, sliced
1 cup canned tomatoes
Salt to taste
Chicken-like broth or seasoning mix to taste

In large skillet, brown rice in oil. Add garlic and onion; cook for 1 minute. Add water and remaining ingredients. Bring to a boil and reduce heat; simmer for about 20 minutes, until rice is cooked.

A TASTE OF LATIN AMERICA

VEGAN

PER SERVING

Calories:	228
Total Fat:	5 g
Cholesterol:	0 mg
Sodium:	56 mg
Carbohydrates:	41 g
Protein:	4 g

CUBA

VEGAN

Cuban Black Beans

LUIS GUTIERREZ

Makes 10 servings

1 pound dry black beans, washed
2 1/2 quarts water
1/2 green pepper, chopped
2 garlic cloves, chopped
1 small onion, chopped
1/3 cup olive oil

1 medium onion, chopped
1 large green pepper, chopped
3 garlic cloves, chopped
1 teaspoon salt
1/2 teaspoon ground cumin
1/2 teaspoon oregano
2 tablespoons vinegar

In a large kettle, soak beans overnight in water.

The next day, add green pepper, garlic, and onion (from first list) and bring to a boil. Reduce heat; simmer until beans are tender.

Meanwhile, in a medium skillet over medium-high heat, sauté the onion and green pepper from second list in olive oil for 2 minutes. Add garlic, salt, cumin, and oregano. Cook for 2 more minutes. Add mixture to beans; stir. Cook for 30 minutes longer at a low heat until beans split open; add vinegar.

PER SERVING

Calories:	227
Total Fat:	8 g
Cholesterol:	0 mg
Sodium:	3 mg
Carbohydrates:	30 g
Protein:	10 g

Navidad

Luis Gutierrez remembers eating these beans as part of Christmas celebrations while he was growing up. Navidad (as they called Christmas in Cuba) celebration commenced on December 24. In some Latin American countries, the festivities lasted until January 6.

As do children in many Hispanic countries, Luis remembers the tradition of putting his shoes in a special place in the house, on the hearth if there was a fireplace. Luis would write a letter to one of the three Kings from the biblical account of Jesus' birth, and put the letter inside his shoes hoping to get the toy he wished for.

December 24 was the day when family would gather to celebrate the holiday. Black beans were always served.

A TASTE OF LATIN AMERICA

VEGAN

Pinto Beans

LOIDA MORALES

Makes 12 servings

6 cups water
3 cups pinto beans, rinsed
1 clove garlic
2 tablespoons corn oil
1 cup chopped onion

2 cloves garlic, minced
3 tablespoons diced green bell pepper
1 tablespoon chicken-like broth or seasoning mix
1/8 teaspoon ground cumin
1/4 cup tomato sauce

In a large kettle, add beans and 1 clove garlic to 6 cups water. Let sit overnight.

In the morning, drain water from beans, keeping garlic clove. Place drained beans and garlic in crock pot. Fill with 6 cups of water. Turn crockpot on high; cook for 8 hours.

In a 4-quart kettle over medium-high heat, sauté onion, minced garlic, and pepper in oil. Add chicken-like seasoning, cumin, and tomato sauce. Pour the cooked beans and liquid into the kettle of vegetables (discard garlic clove); simmer on low for one hour stirring every 5 to 7 minutes. *(The more you stir the beans, the thicker they will become. If you want to use the beans for haystacks, simmer for less time and do not stir them constantly.)*

This recipe may seem time consuming, but it is not. I guarantee these beans will look and taste like you have added real cream to the recipe. The best I have ever had. Our family likes them served over rice, but they are a wonderful accompaniment to any Latin-American entrée.

Loida is from Nicaragua; her husband, Carlos, from Guatemala. She says she never saw pinto beans until she came to the United States. This dish came out of her rich experience cooking foods from the United States and several Latin-American countries.

PER SERVING

Calories:	192
Total Fat:	3 g
Cholesterol:	0 mg
Sodium:	188 mg
Carbohydrates:	32 g
Protein:	10 g

Chicken Fajitas (fah·HEE·tuhs)

Makes 6 servings

2 tablespoons canola oil
1 medium onion, sliced
1 medium green pepper, sliced
1 12.5-ounce can *Worthington® FriChik®*, drained and sliced

1/2 cup sliced fresh mushrooms (stems removed)
1/4 cup water
1 1.12-oz package fajita seasoning mix
6 10-inch flour tortillas

In large skillet over medium heat, sauté the onion and green pepper in oil. When they are almost tender, add mushrooms; continue cooking until tender. Add *FriChik®;* heat through. Add 1/4 cup water, then fajita mix. Continue cooking for 3 more minutes. *Mixture will thicken.* Serve with warm tortillas.

SERVING SUGGESTION: Fajitas can be served with sour cream and/or salsa. Try Debby's Salsa (p. 146).

MEXICO

VEGAN

PER SERVING

Calories:	231
Total Fat:	10 g
Cholesterol:	0 mg
Sodium:	654 mg
Carbohydrates:	24 g
Protein:	8 g

*Fajita seasoning can be found in the packaged seasoning section of your grocery store.

TEX-MEX

Haystacks

Makes 10 to 12 servings

1 13- or 14-ounce bag corn chips*
1 50-ounce can *Worthington® Chili*
   or 1 20-ounce can *Worthington® Chili*
     mixed with a 30-ounce can chili beans (your choice)
   or 1 recipe of Loida's Beans (see p. 96)
1 head iceberg lettuce or leaf lettuce, washed, cored,
   and finely shredded or chopped

6 large tomatoes, washed and cut into pieces
2 pounds cheese, shredded (about 1/2 cup per person)
2 large cans black olives, drained and sliced
1 medium onion, chopped
1 cup guacamole   ⎤ *these measurements are approxi-*
1 cup salsa   ⎥ *mate, it is recommended you*
1 cup sour cream ⎦ *have plenty of each on hand*

Haystacks are a staple of Adventist potlucks and school cafeterias. But in case you don't know, here's how it works: Put a layer of chips on your plate. Add a layer of chili or beans. Then pile on the other ingredients in whatever order you prefer.

AUTHOR'S NOTE: Since everyone "builds" a Haystack differently, I did not want to venture nutritional analysis of this "recipe." For less fat, go easy on the corn chips, canned chili, cheese, guacamole, olives, and sour cream (you can use a fat-free or low-fat sour cream). Load up on the salad ingredients.

*Some people use rice and even cornbread to replace the corn chips, then stack all the other goodies on top.

Salsa-topped Potatoes

Makes 8 servings

4 *Morningstar Farms® Grillers®*, cut into strips
2 cups salsa
2 teaspoons chili powder
2/3 cup water
4 medium baking potatoes, scrubbed and baked

In a medium saucepan over low heat, combine *Grillers®*, salsa, chili powder, and water; cook until thoroughly warmed.

To serve, cut baked potatoes in half and place in a 9" x 13" baking dish. Mash potatoes down slightly. Spoon salsa mixture over potatoes. Bake at 325°F for 15 to 20 minutes, until warmed through.

SERVING SUGGESTION: Serve with a dollop of fat-free sour cream or fat-free plain yogurt.

TEX-MEX

PER SERVING

Calories:	145
Total Fat:	4 g
Cholesterol:	0 mg
Sodium:	309 mg
Carbohydrates:	19 g
Protein:	9 g

Vegetables

Cajun Potato Wedges

Makes 10 servings

2 tablespoons olive oil
6 medium potatoes, cut into wedges or chunks
1 to 2 teaspoons Cajun spice

Preheat oven to 375°F. Pour oil into a 9" x 13" baking dish or onto a medium jelly roll pan. Place in the oven for about 5 minutes (until oil is hot.) Remove pan from oven; place potatoes in it and sprinkle Cajun spice over them. Toss potatoes to coat with oil. Bake 20 to 25 minutes, turning occasionally. They should be golden brown. Serve hot with salsa and sour cream if desired.

You can make this as spicy hot as you like just by adding more Cajun spice. This spice goes a lonnnnnng way!

PER SERVING

Calories:	195
Total Fat:	3 g
Cholesterol:	0 mg
Sodium:	56 mg
Carbohydrates:	40 g
Protein:	4 g

ITALY

Carrots With Cilantro

BOB GORTON

Makes 8 servings

2 pounds carrots, peeled and julienned*
Salt to taste
1/4 cup butter
1/2 cup whole milk
1 teaspoon chopped fresh cilantro

Fill a medium saucepan three-quarters full of water. Bring to a rolling boil; add carrots. Add salt to taste; cook partially covered for 10 minutes or until carrots are tender. Drain; return carrots to saucepan.

In a large skillet over medium-high heat, combine butter, milk and cilantro; heat until butter is melted. Add carrots; fry just long enough for butter and milk to be absorbed. Season to taste. Remove and serve hot.

Don't let this recipe fool you. It looks too simple to be good, but you will really enjoy the new taste of carrots!

PER SERVING

Calories:	103
Total Fat:	6 g
Cholesterol:	17 mg
Sodium:	101 mg
Carbohydrates:	11 g
Protein:	2 g

*See glossary for definition.

Carrottes au Cumin

CELESTE PERRINO WALKER

Makes 8 servings

1 tablespoon olive oil*
3 pounds carrots, peeled and chopped
Salt to taste
3 cloves garlic, chopped
1 teaspoon cumin seed, ground with mortar and pestle**

In a large skillet, sauté chopped carrots in oil for fifteen minutes; salt to taste. Add garlic and cumin. Add a little water, cover; cook over low heat for 45 minutes. Stir frequently so carrots don't burn. Serve hot.

FRANCE

*Celeste uses garlic oil in place of the olive oil. Garlic oil can be found in the Oriental section of most grocery stores.

**See glossary for definition.

PER SERVING

Calories:	81
Total Fat:	2 g
Cholesterol:	0 mg
Sodium:	53 mg
Carbohydrates:	16 g
Protein:	2 g

CHILE

Choclo Esponjoso (CHOH·kloh es·pon·HOH·soh) [Fluffy Corn]

SONIA B. HUNT

Makes 10 servings

7 cups frozen corn, thawed
4 eggs, separated (discard 1 yolk)
1 cup milk
Salt to taste
2 tablespoons powdered sugar

In a medium bowl, combine corn, 3 egg yolks, milk, and salt; stir well.

In a small bowl, beat 4 egg whites with an electric mixer until they hold stiff peaks. Fold gently into corn mixture. Pour into a greased casserole dish; bake at 300°F for 20 minutes.

PER SERVING
Calories:	146
Total Fat:	3 g
Cholesterol:	67 mg
Sodium:	39 mg
Carbohydrates:	27 g
Protein:	6 g

 Onion Pie

Makes 15 servings

ITALY

2 1/2 cups unbleached flour	1/2 cup margarine
1 tablespoon sugar	6 ounces pitted black olives, chopped
1 cup shortening	3/4 cup grated Parmesan cheese
1/4 teaspoon salt	2 tablespoons unbleached flour
2 eggs, beaten	1/2 teaspoon garlic powder
1 1/2 teaspoons cider vinegar	1/4 teaspoon black pepper
4 pounds onions, thinly sliced	1 1/2 teaspoons milk

In a medium bowl, add sugar and salt to 2 1/2 cups flour; mix well. Cut shortening into flour until it resembles coarse crumbs.

In a measuring cup, add enough cold water to 2 tablespoons of beaten egg to make 1/2 cup. To water and egg mixture add vinegar. Stir liquid into flour mixture; mix until it forms a ball. Separate off 1/3 of ball. Set both aside.

In an 8-quart kettle over medium-high heat, sauté 1/2 of the onion in margarine for 5 minutes. Add remaining onion; cook another 5 minutes or until tender. Remove from heat; add olives, cheese, 2 tablespoons flour, garlic powder, pepper, and remaining egg. Stir until blended.

Roll out larger dough ball to fit a 9" x 12" baking dish—it should be thin enough to leave dough hanging over edges. Pour in onion mixture. Roll remaining dough to fit top of dish. Cover onion mixture with top crust and roll edges of bottom dough over to seal. Cut slits in top crust to allow steam to escape. Brush crust with milk before baking. Bake in a 350°F oven for one hour. Crust should be golden brown. *Place foil over edges if they begin to turn too brown.* Remove from oven and let stand 20 minutes. Can be served warm or cold.

PER SERVING

Calories:	350
Total Fat:	23 g
Cholesterol:	33 mg
Sodium:	312 mg
Carbohydrates:	29 g
Protein:	7 g

MEXICO

Mexican Hominy

Makes 12 servings

6 cups canned white hominy, drained
1 cup plain nonfat yogurt*
1 cup sour cream
1/4 teaspoon salt

1 4-ounce can diced green chilies
16 ounces Monterey Jack cheese, grated
Hot sauce to taste

In a large bowl, combine all ingredients; mix well. Bake at 305°F for 45 minutes in a casserole dish covered with foil. Remove foil for last 15 minutes of baking.

If you like hominy, this will be a favorite.

PER SERVING

Calories:	254
Total Fat:	16 g
Cholesterol:	42 mg
Sodium:	446 mg
Carbohydrates:	15 g
Protein:	12 g

*Lite Version note: The original recipe called for 2 cups sour cream. Substituting 1 cup plain nonfat yogurt gives the dish a tangy flavor. You might want to experiment with non-fat sour cream as well.

A Mexican Holiday

PASTOR ARMANDO JUAREZ

The celebration of Cinco de Mayo (May 5) is the third most important in Mexico after Independence Day on September 16 and the November 20 Revolution Day. Cinco de Mayo, however, is the biggest Mexican celebration in the United States. Cinco de Mayo is celebrated in the United States with parades, folk dancing, speeches, carnival rides, and Mexican music.

Cinco de May is actually a commemoration of a victory by Mexican troops in the Battle of Puebla on May 5, 1862. At that time, the French Army of Napoleon III was considered the premier army in the world. It had enjoyed recent victories throughout Europe and Asia. The Mexican army, led by General Ignacio Zaragoza, won the battle even though the French force was better armed and twice as large. It is a story like David defeating Goliath.

Since its independence from Spain in 1821, Mexico had suffered one tragedy after another. Many historians say that after the failure of this attempt to tamper with Mexico's sovereignty, Mexican nationalism and self-esteem began to grow perceptibly for the first time in history. This May 5 battle has come to symbolize the strength and determination of the Mexican people and is celebrated every year as Cinco de Mayo.

For me, Cinco de Mayo has a parallel with Calvary. Before knowing Christ, my life was one "tragedy" after another. But, after I met Christ, my self-esteem, my strength, and my determination were changed and now I am able to face difficult situations. With Christ I am a winner.

PHILIPPINES

Pancit Bijon (PAHN·sit bee·JON)

CAROL DODGE

Makes 8 servings

2 eggs, beaten
3 tablespoons canola oil
1/2 cup sliced onion
1/2 cup sliced fresh mushrooms
1 cup sliced celery
1/2 cup thinly sliced carrots

1 cup shredded cabbage
1/2 teaspoon salt
5 tablespoons lite soy sauce
3/4 cup warm water
1 8-ounce package rice sticks*

In a medium skillet over medium heat, with half of the canola oil, scramble the eggs until dry. Remove from heat and set aside.

With remaining oil in another medium fry pan over medium-high heat, sauté onion, celery, and mushrooms for 2 minutes. Add carrots and cook 2 more minutes; then add cabbage. Add seasonings and water to vegetable mixture.

Break rice sticks apart and soak in boiling water for 10 seconds. (After being soaked in water, rice sticks resemble translucent spaghetti.) Drain and add to hot vegetable mixture. Simmer gently until vegetables and rice sticks are tender. Add scrambled eggs and serve with lemon or lime juice.

SERVING SUGGESTION: You may scramble fresh or frozen tofu in place of eggs and may add 1 small can tomato sauce if desired.

*See glossary for definition.

PER SERVING

Calories:	158
Total Fat:	6 g
Cholesterol:	54 mg
Sodium:	848 mg
Carbohydrates:	21 g
Protein:	3 g

Peppery Green Beans With Coconut

Makes 6 servings

2 tablespoons canola oil
1 teaspoon mustard seed*
1 small onion, chopped
1 teaspoon minced fresh gingerroot
1/4 teaspoon cayenne pepper
1 pound fresh green beans, trimmed and cubed

1 medium red pepper, sliced
1/2 cup water
1 cup whole corn
1/4 cup unsweetened or sweetened shredded coconut
1 1/2 tablespoons lemon juice concentrate

**A TASTE OF
THE ORIENT**

In a large skillet over medium-high heat, fry mustard seeds in oil until they pop. Stir in onion and ginger; cook for 2 minutes. Stir in cayenne pepper, beans, pepper, and water; cook for 3 minutes or until beans are tender. Stir in corn, coconut, and lemon juice; heat for 1 minute.

A nice change from regular green beans.

*If you have never used whole mustard seed before, you might want to cover your pan when they begin to pop. They escape like popcorn if left uncovered. However, they will burn if you aren't careful, so you have to both cover them and watch them!

PER SERVING

Calories:	166
Total Fat:	11 g
Cholesterol:	0 mg
Sodium:	14 mg
Carbohydrates:	16 g
Protein:	3 g

INDIA

Potato Curry

Makes 8 servings

1 tablespoon oil
1 teaspoon mustard seeds
2 medium onions, chopped
1 teaspoon chopped fresh garlic
1 teaspoon turmeric
1 teaspoon chopped fresh ginger

1 medium green chili, seeded and chopped
1 pound white potatoes, boiled, peeled,
    and cut into large chunks
Salt to taste
3 tablespoons fresh cilantro leaves, finely chopped

In a large skillet over medium-high heat, sauté mustard seeds in oil. When they begin to crack, add onion and garlic; sauté for 2 minutes. Add turmeric, ginger, and chili; fry for 2 to 3 minutes to let the flavors mix, then add potatoes. Salt to taste; fry for 2 to 3 more minutes. Sprinkle with cilantro when ready to serve. Serve with Chapatis (see p. 27).

PER SERVING

Calories:	78
Total Fat:	2 g
Cholesterol:	0 mg
Sodium:	6 mg
Carbohydrates:	14 g
Protein:	2 g

Spinach Sauce [Mchicha (mee·CHEE·cha)]

JAYMEE FRIMML

TANZANIA

Makes 6 servings

1/4 cup chopped onion
1 tablespoon canola oil
1 10-ounce package frozen chopped spinach,
    thawed and drained

1 teaspoon salt
1 16-ounce can diced or stewed tomatoes
1 green chili, finely chopped

In a medium skillet over medium-high heat, sauté onion in oil until tender. Add spinach and salt; cook about 10 minutes. Add tomatoes and chili; bring to a boil. Reduce heat; simmer, allowing some of the liquid to evaporate.

SERVING SUGGESTION: This is a wonderfully easy-to-prepare Friday evening supper. Serve over brown rice. To make it truly African, sit on the floor on a colorful blanket, and serve it with a thick white corn meal mush. Eat it with your fingers! Place the corn meal mush in a big bowl in the center. Each person dips their middle, ring, and little fingers into the bowl like a scoop, to get some of the cornmeal mush and then dips into their own bowl to add Mchicha. A mouthwatering combination!

PER SERVING

Calories:	56
Total Fat:	2 g
Cholesterol:	0 mg
Sodium:	583 mg
Carbohydrates:	8 g
Protein:	2 g

MEXICO

Sweet Corn Cakes

Makes 10 servings

2 tablespoons shortening
1/4 cup butter
1/2 cup masa (corn flour)
3 tablespoons cold water
1 10-ounce package frozen corn

3 tablespoons cornmeal
1/4 cup sugar
2 tablespoons evaporated milk
1/4 teaspoon baking powder
1/4 teaspoon salt

In small mixing bowl, whip shortening and butter until fluffy and creamy. Gradually add masa, then water; set aside.

In a blender, process corn kernels until coarsely chopped. Stir into masa mixture.

In a large mixing bowl, combine cornmeal, sugar, milk, baking powder, and salt; whip together. Add butter-masa mixture; mix just until blended. Pour into an 8" greased baking dish; cover with foil. Bake in preheated, 350°F oven 40 to 50 minutes or until firm. Let stand at room temperature for 15 minutes. When ready to serve, either cut into squares or scoop with a small ice cream scoop.

This recipe is an adaptation of the corn cakes served at some Mexican restaurants

PER SERVING

Calories:	142
Total Fat:	8 g
Cholesterol:	13 mg
Sodium:	113 mg
Carbohydrates:	17 g
Protein:	2 g

Swiss Eggplant

Makes 6 servings

1 egg, beaten
Flour (for coating)
1 medium eggplant, sliced 1/2" thick
2 tablespoons canola oil
1 20-ounce can diced tomatoes

1 large onion, sliced
1 green pepper, sliced
Salt to taste
1/4 cup unbleached flour
1/4 cup water

Dip eggplant slices in egg, then in flour, coating each side.

In a large skillet over medium-high heat, fry eggplant in oil until golden brown. Remove eggplant from pan; set aside.

In the same skillet, combine tomatoes, onion, green pepper, and salt; bring to a boil. Reduce heat to low. Add eggplant; simmer for 15 minutes or until onion and pepper are tender.

In a small bowl, whisk together 1/4 cup flour and 1/4 cup water until lumps are gone. Pour over eggplant to thicken sauce. Serve hot.

SWITZERLAND

PER SERVING

Calories:	123
Total Fat:	6 g
Cholesterol:	35 mg
Sodium:	168 mg
Carbohydrates:	16 g
Protein:	4 g

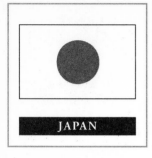

JAPAN

Teriyaki Eggplant Cutlets

Dorothy M. Decker

Makes 10 servings

2 eggplants, chopped
Salt
1 medium onion, diced
2 tablespoons low-sodium soy sauce
2 tablespoons granulated sugar

1/4 teaspoon garlic powder
1/4 teaspoon ground ginger
2 cups fine bread crumbs
1 cup *Morningstar Farms® Scramblers®*

Put eggplant in colander and sprinkle with salt. Let stand for 30 minutes; rinse. Gently squeeze out any remaining water; place eggplant in a medium bowl. Add diced onion.

In a small bowl, mix soy sauce, sugar, garlic powder, and ginger. Sprinkle over eggplant; mix well. Add breadcrumbs; toss. Add *Scramblers®;* mix well. *Mixture will be mushy.* With damp hands, form mixture into small patties.

Spray a large skillet with nonstick cooking spray. Over medium-high heat, fry both sides of patties until golden brown.

PER SERVING

Calories:	137
Total Fat:	1 g
Cholesterol:	0 mg
Sodium:	343 mg
Carbohydrates:	26 g
Protein:	6 g

Zucchini Casserole

BOB GORTON

Makes 15 servings

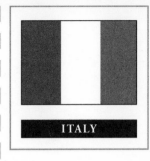

ITALY

1 cup *Morningstar Farms® Scramblers®*
1 teaspoon salt
1 1/2 cups bread crumbs
1 cup grated Parmesan cheese
3 tablespoons finely-chopped fresh basil

1 teaspoon dried thyme
2 tablespoons chopped fresh parsley
2 pounds zucchini, sliced 1/8" thick diagonally
1 pound mozzarella cheese, sliced 1/8" thick
2 Roma tomatoes*, thinly sliced

Preheat oven to 350°F. In a medium mixing bowl, mix *Scramblers®* and salt together.

In a separate mixing bowl, stir together bread crumbs, Parmesan cheese, basil, thyme, and parsley.

Spray bottom of an 11" x 14" baking dish with nonstick cooking spray. Place a layer of zucchini on the bottom. Over that layer put a layer each of sliced mozzarella and sliced tomatoes. Sprinkle 1/4 of bread crumb mixture over the top. Repeat until all ingredients are used *(usually 4 layers)*. Before baking, pour egg mixture evenly over top.

Bake for 45 minutes or until golden brown; egg mixture should be set. Make sure casserole does not brown too quickly—if it does, cover with foil, then remove foil the last five minutes of baking. Remove from oven and wait a few minutes before cutting *(egg will set more firmly)*. Serve hot.

PER SERVING

Calories:	184
Total Fat:	10 g
Cholesterol:	31 mg
Sodium:	486 mg
Carbohydrates:	12 g
Protein:	12 g

Desserts

Sesame Honey Bars [Pastelli]

GREECE

Makes 24 servings

1 cup honey
1 cup sesame seeds

In a medium saucepan, boil honey until it reaches about 250°F on a candy thermometer. *You might need to stir honey down every once in a while as it bubbles up quite rapidly.* Stir in sesame seeds; cook until the seeds are golden in color and the syrup reaches a boil. *The syrup will reach 265°F.*

Spread evenly in a very well-greased 9" x 13" baking dish. When almost cool, cut into small diamond shapes.

This is a very chewy candy, almost to the point of being sticky, but the taste is excellent. You could heat to the Soft Crack Stage on your candy thermometer to achieve a more firm candy.

PER SERVING

Calories:	77
Total Fat:	3 g
Cholesterol:	0 mg
Sodium:	1 mg
Carbohydrates:	13 g
Protein:	1 g

SYRIA

Butter Cookies

Makes 48 servings

2 cups unsalted butter,* softened
3/4 cup powdered sugar
1 egg yolk
1 tablespoon milk

1 teaspoon vanilla extract
4 1/2 cups unbleached flour
1 teaspoon baking powder
Granulated sugar (to coat stamp or glass)

Preheat oven to 350°F. Using an electric mixer, cream butter until lemon-colored. Gradually beat in sugar; blend well. Add egg yolk, milk, and vanilla; beat until mixture is fluffy. Gradually add flour and baking powder; mix well. *The dough should be soft but not sticky.*

Shape into balls; place on an ungreased cookie sheet. Flatten with a cookie stamp or the bottom of a glass; dip stamp or glass in sugar after you press each ball. Bake 10 minutes or until golden brown.

PER SERVING
Calories: 123
Total Fat: 8 g
Cholesterol: 29 mg
Sodium: 9 mg
Carbohydrates: 11 g
Protein: 1 g

*If you substitute margarine for butter you will cut cholesterol, but you will loose the wonderful butter flavor.

Chinese Almond Cookies

Makes 43 servings

3/4 cup shortening
3/4 cup granulated sugar
1 egg
2 tablespoons water
1 teaspoon almond extract

2 1/2 cups unbleached flour
1/4 teaspoon salt
1 teaspoon baking powder
22 whole almonds
Granulated sugar (to coat glass)

CHINA

Preheat oven to 350°F.

With an electric mixer, cream together shortening, sugar, and egg. Add water and almond extract; beat until fluffy. Add flour, salt, and baking powder; mix on low until a stiff batter forms. Refrigerate for one hour. Remove from refrigerator.

Roll dough into 1-inch balls. Place on a greased cookie sheet and flatten to 1/4" with the bottom of a glass; dip glass in sugar after you press each ball. Split whole almonds, press half into each cookie before baking. Bake 10 to 12 minutes, until golden brown. Cool on wire racks.

PER SERVING

Calories:	75
Total Fat:	4 g
Cholesterol:	5 mg
Sodium:	23 mg
Carbohydrates:	9 g
Protein:	1 g

**A TASTE OF
THE ORIENT**

Chinese New Year Cookies

Makes 36 servings

1 6-ounce package semisweet chocolate chips
1 6-ounce package butterscotch morsels
3 ounces chow mein noodles
7 ounces salted peanuts

Place chocolate and butterscotch chips in large glass bowl and microwave for 1 minute on high; stir. If they need to be melted further, microwave for 20 seconds at a time. When the chips have melted completely, mix in chow mein noodles and peanuts. Drop by spoonfuls onto waxed paper and chill.

This chocolate confection is good at a Chinese New Year celebration or any time dessert is served.

PER SERVING

Calories:	81
Total Fat:	4 g
Cholesterol:	0 mg
Sodium:	45 mg
Carbohydrates:	10 g
Protein:	2 g

A Chinese Festival

Mooncakes are an indispensable part of Chinese culture. According to popular belief, the custom of eating mooncakes began in the late Yuan dynasty. As the story goes, the Han people of that time resented the Mongol rule of the Yuan regime, and revolutionaries, led by Chu Yan-chang, plotted to usurp the throne.

Chu needed to find a way of uniting the people to revolt on the same day without letting the Mongol rulers learn of the plan. Chu's close advisor, Liu Po-wen, finally came up with a brilliant idea. A rumor was spread that a plague was ravaging the land and that only by eating a special mooncake distributed by the revolutionaries could the disaster be prevented. The mooncakes were then distributed only to the Han people, who found, upon cutting the cakes open, the message "Revolt on the fifteenth of the eighth moon." Thus informed, the people rose together on the designated day to overthrow the Yuan, and since that time mooncakes have become an integral part of the Mid-Autumn Festival, around September 27.

These golden pastry delicacies come with a variety of fillings which include Durian, a strong onion flavored-tasting fruit found in Asia (and something Ken and I never acquired a taste for while living in Asia), lotus seeds, mixed fruits and nuts, and of course, a single or double salted egg yolk (which really surprises you on your first sampling of a mooncake).

ORDERING INFORMATION: Eastern Bakery in Chinatown, San Francisco, CA; phone: (415) 392-4497

FRANCE

Chocolate-filled Bonbons

Makes 36 servings

3/4 cup shortening
1/2 cup granulated sugar
1/4 cup brown sugar
1 egg
2 teaspoons vanilla extract
1/2 teaspoon almond extract

1 3/4 cups unbleached flour
1/2 teaspoon baking powder
1/2 teaspoon salt
1/2 cup finely chopped pecans
36 bite-sized solid milk chocolate candies
Powdered sugar

With an electric mixer cream together shortening, sugar, egg, vanilla, and almond extract. Add flour, baking powder, salt, and pecans; mix well.

Shape dough into 36 balls. Press each ball around a chocolate candy, covering it completely. Place on a greased cookie sheet; bake in a 350°F oven for 12 to 14 minutes. Remove and roll in powdered sugar. Cool on a wire rack.

PER SERVING

Calories:	134
Total Fat:	8 g
Cholesterol:	6 mg
Sodium:	38 mg
Carbohydrates:	15 g
Protein:	1 g

Dutch Bon Ket*

STEVE A. HILDE

Makes 48 servings

2 cups unbleached flour
1/2 cup shortening
1/2 cup butter
1/2 cup iced water

1/2 cup marzipan**
1 cup sugar
1/4 cup egg substitute
1 tablespoon vanilla extract

FRANCE

In a large bowl, mix flour, shortening, butter, and iced water just as you would for a pie crust. Put in freezer until filling is ready.

In a small bowl, blend marzipan, sugar, egg, and vanilla until smooth. Small lumps are acceptable. *(I used an electric beater. Marzipan tends to be quite solid.)*

Roll crust into two 4" wide rectangular strips. Put filling down center of one rectangle. Before the filling spreads, fold dough over and pinch edges and ends; make sure it is sealed tightly. Repeat for second strip. Transfer to an ungreased cookie sheet; bake at 325°F for 35 minutes. Cool; cut diagonally.

These are exceptionally flavored, and very pretty to use for special occasions.

*The contributor notes: "This recipe was handed down from my French grandmother who was married to a Zeelander."

**See glossary for definition.

PER SERVING

Calories:	83
Total Fat:	4 g
Cholesterol:	10 mg
Sodium:	21 mg
Carbohydrates:	10 g
Protein:	1 g

A TASTE OF THE ORIENT

These cookies are a Chinese-American invention and are often served after a meal in Chinese-American restaurants.

PER SERVING

Calories:	48
Total Fat:	3 g
Cholesterol:	0 mg
Sodium:	6 mg
Carbohydrates:	5 g
Protein:	1 g

Fortune Cookies

Makes 10 servings

1/4 cup cake flour
2 tablespoons granulated sugar
1 tablespoon cornstarch
2 tablespoons canola oil

1 egg white
1 tablespoon water*
Dash of salt

Before starting cookies, write fortunes on small slips of paper (2" x 3/8" works well).

In a small bowl, mix all ingredients together until smooth. Drop by one teaspoon at a time into a hot skillet; cook both sides. Remove from skillet; while still warm, place paper fortune in the middle of cookie. Fold cookie in half, then bend in the middle of the straight side, pinching ends together to form shape of a fortune cookie.

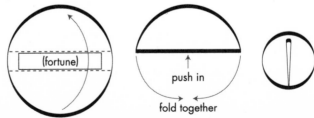

*You might want to experiment with thinning the batter with more water. These cookies tend to be a little thicker and chewier than what you might get in a Chinese restaurant.

Funnel Cakes

Makes 6 servings

1 1/4 cups unbleached flour
2 tablespoons granulated sugar
1 teaspoon baking soda
3/4 teaspoon baking powder
1/4 teaspoon salt

1 egg
3/4 cup 1 % milk
Canola oil (for frying)
2 teaspoons powdered sugar

NETHERLANDS

In a large bowl, combine dry ingredients; mix. Add egg and milk; beat until smooth.

In a large skillet, heat 1/4" oil to 375°F. Cover the bottom opening of a funnel with your finger. Pour 1/4 cup batter into the funnel; hold over the center of the skillet. Remove finger from funnel end; as batter begins to flow, move funnel in a circular motion to form a spiral. *Stop flow of batter when funnel cake is large enough by placing finger back over the funnel opening.*

Fry 2 minutes or until golden brown, turning once. Drain on a paper towel; sprinkle with powdered sugar. Serve hot with maple syrup, if desired.

PER SERVING

Calories:	200
Total Fat:	8 g
Cholesterol:	37 mg
Sodium:	370 mg
Carbohydrates:	26 g
Protein:	5 g

GERMANY

Banana German Chocolate Cake

Makes 15 servings

1 package German chocolate cake mix
1 1/4 cup mashed ripe bananas
1 cup water
1/3 cup canola oil
3 eggs

1 16-ounce can pre-made coconut-pecan frosting
1 1-ounce square unsweetened chocolate, melted
1/2 cup powdered sugar
2 teaspoons water

With an electric mixer, beat cake mix, 1 cup bananas, water, oil, and eggs at low speed until moistened, scraping sides and bottom of bowl while mixing. Beat at high speed for 2 minutes until fluffy. Pour batter into greased 9" x 13" cake pan. Bake at 350°F for 30 to 40 minutes, until a knife inserted into the center of the cake comes out clean. Cool completely.

In a small bowl, combine ready-made frosting and remaining 1/4 cup mashed banana. Stir well; spread over cooled cake.

In a small bowl, combine melted chocolate, powdered sugar, and water. *The glaze should be thin enough to drizzle on cake.* Drizzle over frosting with a small spoon. Store cake in refrigerator until ready to serve.

PER SERVING

Calories:	317
Total Fat:	16 g
Cholesterol:	43 mg
Sodium:	287 mg
Carbohydrates:	43 g
Protein:	3 g

German Chocolate Upside Down Cake

BECKY OWENS

Makes 15 servings

GERMANY

1 cup shredded coconut
1 cup chopped pecans
1 package German chocolate cake mix,
    prepared according to package directions—unbaked
1 8-ounce package cream cheese
1/2 cup margarine
1 pound powdered sugar

Spread coconut and pecans evenly in the bottom of a greased 9" x 13" baking pan. Pour prepared cake mix over coconut and pecans.

In a small saucepan or in microwave at low heat, melt margarine and cream cheese. Stir in powdered sugar until well blended; pour over cake mix. Bake at 350°F for 40 to 50 minutes, until a knife, inserted into the center of the cake, comes out clean. *(Cream cheese mixture will fall to the bottom of the baking dish while baking.)*

PER SERVING
Calories: 442
Total Fat: 26 g
Cholesterol: 60 mg
Sodium: 345 mg
Carbohydrates: 51 g
Protein: 4 g

MEXICO

Pastel de Piña

Makes 15 servings

1 20-ounce can crushed pineapple, undrained
2 cups unbleached flour
2 teaspoons baking soda
2 cups granulated sugar
2 eggs

1 cup chopped walnuts
2 cups powdered sugar
1/2 cup margarine
1 8-ounce package lowfat cream cheese

In a large bowl, combine pineapple, flour, baking soda, granulated sugar, eggs, and walnuts. Pour into a greased 9" x 13" cake pan and bake at 350° F for 45 minutes or until top is golden.

FROSTING: In a medium bowl, combine powdered sugar, margarine, and cream cheese. Frost cake while it is still hot.

PER SERVING

Calories:	398
Total Fat:	14 g
Cholesterol:	37 mg
Sodium:	354 mg
Carbohydrates:	63 g
Protein:	6 g

Rice Cake*

CAROL DODGE

Makes 15 servings

2 cups rice flour**
1 1/2 cup brown sugar
1 1/2 cups shredded coconut
3 eggs
2 cups 1% milk

1 teaspoon baking powder
1 cup brown sugar
1 1/2 cups shredded coconut
1/2 cup margarine, melted

PHILIPPINES

With an electric mixer, beat together flour, 1 1/2 cups brown sugar, 1 1/2 cups coconut, eggs, milk, and baking powder. Bake at 350°F in greased 9" x 13" cake pan for 28 minutes, until almost done. Remove from oven.

FROSTING: In a medium saucepan over medium heat, cook 1 cup brown sugar and 1 1/2 cups coconut in melted margarine for 3 minutes, stirring constantly. Pour over almost-baked cake and place back in oven at 250°F for 10 to 12 more minutes.

AUTHOR'S NOTE: I prefer baking the cake until done, 35 to 40 minutes. Remove from oven; spread coconut frosting over cake. The topping will be softer this way. When it is spread on top and continues baking with the cake, it thickens more. Either way it is good.

*This recipe uses no wheat flour, so is acceptable for someone with wheat allergies. You can also use a non-dairy milk product to replace the milk.

**Rice flour can be found in many large supermarkets and any health food store.

PER SERVING	
Calories:	390
Total Fat:	14 g
Cholesterol:	44 mg
Sodium:	187 mg
Carbohydrates:	63 g
Protein:	4 g

ITALY

Italian Prune Pie

BLANCHE FISHER

Makes 8 servings

3 1/2 cups Italian prunes, seeded and quartered
1/2 cup granulated sugar
1/4 cup unbleached flour
1/4 teaspoon salt
1 tablespoon lemon juice concentrate

1/3 cup margarine
3/4 cup unbleached flour
1/2 cup granulated sugar

1 9-inch, unbaked pie crust

In a large bowl, toss prunes, 1/2 cup sugar, 1/4 cup flour, salt, and lemon juice. Set aside.

TOPPING: In a small bowl, cut margarine into 3/4 cup flour and 1/2 cup sugar until the mixture resembles coarse crumbs.

Spread prune mixture evenly into prepared pie crust. Sprinkle topping over prune mixture. Bake at 425°F for 10 minutes. Turn oven to 350°F and bake another 40 minutes or until tender.

This is an exceptional recipe. I got it from Blanche back in the 60s and have made it every year when Italian prunes are in season. You will enjoy the flavors.

PER SERVING

Calories:	391
Total Fat:	14 g
Cholesterol:	0 mg
Sodium:	235 mg
Carbohydrates:	64 g
Protein:	4 g

Swedish Apple Pie

Makes 8 servings

4 cups apple slices
1/4 cup water
2 tablespoons flour
3/4 cup granulated sugar
Pinch of salt
1 egg
1 teaspoon vanilla extract

1 cup sour cream
1 unbaked 9" pie crust
1/2 cup granulated sugar
1/2 cup flour
1 teaspoon ground cinnamon
1/3 cup brown sugar
1/2 cup margarine

SWEDEN

In a large saucepan over low heat, cook apples in water. When soft, drain; mash apples slightly. Add flour, 3/4 cup sugar, and salt.

In a small bowl, mix egg, vanilla, and sour cream. Add to apple mixture. Pour into the unbaked pie shell; bake at 350°F for 40 minutes.

TOPPING: In medium bowl, combine remaining 1/2 cup sugar and 1/2 cup flour with cinnamon, brown sugar, and margarine. Mix with a pastry blender until it resembles coarse crumbs. Remove pie from oven; sprinkle with topping. Bake another 15 minutes.

PER SERVING

Calories:	498
Total Fat:	24 g
Cholesterol:	39 mg
Sodium:	306 mg
Carbohydrates:	68 g
Protein:	4 g

GERMANY

Bavarian Honey Lemon Pudding

Marcy Ainsworth

Makes 8 servings

1 3-ounce package lemon gelatin
1 1/4 cups hot water
1/4 cup honey
1/4 teaspoon salt

1/2 teaspoon vanilla extract
1/4 teaspoon almond extract
1 cup heavy whipping cream, whipped

In a medium bowl, dissolve lemon gelatin in hot water. Add honey and salt; place in refrigerator until thick, but not firm. Remove from refrigerator and add vanilla, almond extract, and whipped cream; fold in gently. Pour into individual dessert bowls; return to refrigerator to set. Serve chilled.

PER SERVING

Calories:	176
Total Fat:	11 g
Cholesterol:	41 mg
Sodium:	106 mg
Carbohydrates:	19 g
Protein:	1 g

Crème Brûlée (krehm broo·LAY)

FRANCE

Makes 8 servings

1 3-ounce package vanilla instant pudding mix
1 1/2 cups skim milk
2 fresh pears (optional)
1 10-ounce package frozen raspberries, thawed and drained
2 cups lite sour cream
1/2 cup brown sugar

In a medium bowl, whisk together pudding mix and milk. Pour into a shallow 1-quart baking dish. Refrigerate until firm.

When ready to serve, peel and thinly slice the fresh pears; arrange on top of pudding. Top with raspberries. Spread sour cream evenly over fruit; sprinkle with brown sugar. Turn oven on broil. Broil 3 inches from element for 1 to 2 minutes. *Sugar will caramelize.*

PER SERVING

Calories:	199
Total Fat:	3 g
Cholesterol:	11 mg
Sodium:	196 mg
Carbohydrates:	43 g
Protein:	3 g

COLOMBIA

Flan (FLAHN)

Ilva Penalosa

Makes 8 servings

3 tablespoons sugar
4 eggs*
1 can sweetened condensed milk (not evaporated milk)

1 can 1% milk—measure in sweetened condensed milk can
1 teaspoon vanilla extract

In the top of a double boiler, directly over medium-high heat, melt sugar and burn slightly. Remove from heat and swirl pan to coat with melted sugar. Set in refrigerator until hard.

In a medium mixing bowl combine eggs, milks, and vanilla; whip until mixed. Remove top double boiler pan from refrigerator; pour milk mixture over crystallized sugar. Fill the bottom part of the double boiler with water; bring to a boil over medium-high heat. Reduce heat until water is at a rolling boil; place top of the double boiler (with milk mixture) over boiling water. Cover with lid; cook for 45 minutes or until center is firm. Remove top pan from double boiler; place in refrigerator until cool. When ready to serve, remove from refrigerator; gently swirl pan in circular motion, loosening custard from sides of pan. Place a dish over the top of the pan; quickly turn over. *The flan will fall into the dish and believe it or not, the caramelized sugar is now the wonderful-tasting, liquid part of the flan.*

Another name for this dessert is Baño Maria (Maria's Bath).

*Lite version substitution: Using 1 cup *Morningstar Farms® Scramblers®* instead of whole eggs reduces fat to 3 grams/serving and cholesterol to 13 grams/serving.

PER SERVING

Calories:	168
Total Fat:	4 g
Cholesterol:	14 mg
Sodium:	107 mg
Carbohydrates:	27 g
Protein:	6 g

Leopard-Spots Ice Cream

Makes 10 servings

1 quart vanilla ice cream, softened
1 cup peanut butter

A TASTE OF AFRICA

Using 1 tablespoon at a time, fold peanut butter into ice cream. *This gives the effect of leopard spots.* Refreeze until ready to serve.

SERVING SUGGESTION: When serving, be sure to scoop into a glass or clear bowl so you can see the leopard spots. Top with chocolate syrup if you wish.

PER SERVING

Calories:	257
Total Fat:	19 g
Cholesterol:	23 mg
Sodium:	166 mg
Carbohydrates:	18 g
Protein:	8 g

AUSTRALIA

Pavlova

JAN JUDD

Makes 10 servings

4 egg whites (at room temperature)
1 cup granulated sugar
1 1/2 teaspoons cornstarch
1 teaspoon lemon juice

Preheat oven to 250°F. With an electric mixer, beat egg whites until they hold stiff peaks. Gradually add sugar and cornstarch a few tablespoons at a time, beating continually until all the sugar has been added and has dissolved. Fold in lemon juice.

Lightly grease a cookie sheet. Lay a sheet of baking parchment on cookie sheet; grease parchment paper as well. Spread egg white mixture on parchment paper to the size of a dinner plate. Smooth the top; bake 2 hours. *Do not open oven door during baking time.* Allow to cool before attempting to remove paper.

SERVING SUGGESTION: Decorate with whipped cream and fruit. Australians usually use sliced bananas, peaches, strawberries, and passion fruit. Use lots of fruit.

PER SERVING

Calories:	86
Total Fat:	0 g
Cholesterol:	0 mg
Sodium:	22 mg
Carbohydrates:	20 g
Protein:	1 g

Raspberry Kissel

MARY SCHWANTES

Makes 8 servings

3 12-ounce packages frozen raspberries
1 cup water
4 1/2 teaspoons cornstarch
1/4 cup cold water
1/2 cup half and half
Sugar to taste

RUSSIA/UKRAINE

In a large saucepan over medium heat, bring raspberries and 1 cup water to a slow boil; simmer until berries are soft. Place berries in a sieve and allow juice to drain into a bowl; discard seeds. Taste liquid; add sugar if necessary (bearing in mind that kissel should be tart.) Return berry juice to stove over medium-high heat.

In a small bowl dissolve cornstarch in 1/4 cup cold water; stir to remove lumps. Stir into hot berry liquid; bring just to a boil. Boil until thickened. Remove from heat and pour into 8 dessert cups. Cover each cup with plastic wrap; chill. Serve cold with 1 tablespoon half and half.

This light, delicate dessert is perfect after a heavy meal.

PER SERVING

Calories:	151
Total Fat:	2 g
Cholesterol:	6 mg
Sodium:	9 mg
Carbohydrates:	34 g
Protein:	1 g

Miscellaneous

Corn Soup

JOCELYN FAY

Makes 10 servings

4 dried Chinese mushrooms
1 medium onion, chopped
1 tablespoon grated gingerroot
8 ounces firm tofu
2 10.2-ounce cans condensed cream of mushroom
    soup, undiluted

1 15-ounce can creamed corn
1/2 cup finely-chopped cilantro
Salt to taste

CHINA

Soak dried mushrooms in hot water. When they are soft, squeeze dry and slice into thin slivers. Reserve liquid.

In a medium kettle, sauté onion, mushrooms, and ginger in a small amount of oil until onion is soft. Mash tofu with fork; add to onion mixture. Add mushroom soup, creamed corn, and enough water (including mushroom water) until soup is desired consistency; heat through. Add cilantro and salt to taste. Serve hot.

PER SERVING

Calories:	110
Total Fat:	5 g
Cholesterol:	1 mg
Sodium:	482 mg
Carbohydrates:	14 g
Protein:	4 g

FINLAND

Finnish Vegetable Soup

Makes 8 servings

2 cups water
2 small carrots, sliced
1 medium potato, cubed
3/4 cup frozen green peas
1 cup frozen green beans
1/4 cup cauliflower flowerets

2 cups fresh spinach, washed thoroughly and chopped
2 tablespoons unbleached flour
2 cups 1% milk
1/4 cup evaporated milk
1 1/2 teaspoons salt

In a 3-quart pot over medium-high heat, bring water, carrots, potato, peas, beans, and cauliflower to a boil. Reduce heat; simmer 10 minutes or until vegetables are tender. Add spinach.

In a small bowl, stir together 1/4 cup milk and flour until all lumps dissolve. Add to vegetable mixture; boil for one minute. Stir in remaining 1 3/4 cups milk, evaporated milk, and salt. Heat until hot; serve.

PER SERVING

Calories:	105
Total Fat:	1 g
Cholesterol:	5 mg
Sodium:	477 mg
Carbohydrates:	19 g
Protein:	5 g

Refried Bean Soup

PAT GILBERT

Makes 10 servings

A TASTE OF LATIN AMERICA

1/4 cup margarine
1 medium onion, chopped fine
2 16-ounce cans refried beans
2 cans condensed tomato soup, undiluted
1 cup evaporated milk

1 cup water
1/4 teaspoon garlic salt
1 teaspoon chili powder
1/2 teaspoon paprika
Salt to taste

In a large saucepan over medium-high heat, sauté onion in margarine until tender. Add remaining ingredients; season to taste. Reduce heat; heat slowly so it does not scorch.

This is a hearty soup that is best served with French bread or garlic bread. Yum!

VARIATION: Add part of a package of a chili mix for more flavor.

PER SERVING

Calories:	225
Total Fat:	8 g
Cholesterol:	9 mg
Sodium:	998 mg
Carbohydrates:	30 g
Protein:	9 g

ITALY

Roman Holiday Soup

MICHELE DEPPE

Makes 12 servings

4 cloves garlic, minced
4 tablespoons butter
29 ounces vegetable broth
1 14 1/2-ounce can stewed and chopped tomatoes

1 10-ounce package frozen spinach, cooked
1 10-ounce package cheese-filled tortellini*
1/2 teaspoon dried oregano
1/2 teaspoon dried parsley

In large 4 quart saucepan over medium-high heat, sauté garlic in butter till golden. Add remaining ingredients; simmer for about 15 minutes or until pasta is tender. Serve soup in individual bowls; sprinkle with freshly grated Parmesan before serving.

PER SERVING

Calories:	150
Total Fat:	6 g
Cholesterol:	27 mg
Sodium:	600 mg
Carbohydrates:	18 g
Protein:	6 g

*Michele has used fresh and frozen cheese-filled tortellini as well as dried. Because different types and sizes of pasta absorb different amounts of liquid, more broth may be needed.

Tortellini & Bean Soup

Makes 8 servings

8 cups vegetable broth
1 medium onion, diced
1 cup diced celery
1/2 pound fresh green beans, trimmed and cubed
1 teaspoon chopped fresh garlic

2 medium zucchini, chopped
1 medium sweet potato, peeled and diced
15 ounces fresh or frozen cheese-filled tortellini
1 pound spinach leaves, washed
1 15-ounce can navy beans

ITALY

In a 4-quart pot, bring broth, onion, celery, green beans, and garlic to a boil. Reduce heat; simmer for 5 minutes, until green beans are tender. Add zucchini, sweet potato, and tortellini; simmer until zucchini, sweet potato, and tortellini are tender, about 5 minutes. Stir in chopped spinach and navy beans; cook for another 5 minutes; serve.

PER SERVING

Calories:	210
Total Fat:	3 g
Cholesterol:	11 mg
Sodium:	1184 mg
Carbohydrates:	32 g
Protein:	15 g

GUATEMALA

Chirmol Sauce [Hot Sauce]

Makes 12 servings

4 tablespoons chopped fresh cilantro
1 28-ounce canned crushed tomatoes
2/3 cup water
1 teaspoon salt
2 teaspoons dried onions
1 teaspoon crushed chiles de arbol*

In a medium bowl, mix all ingredients together.

SERVING SUGGESTION: Enjoy as a dip or on top of fried or baked eggs, with refried beans . . . the possibilities are endless.

VARIATIONS: You may wish to use fresh tomatoes when they are so plentiful during the summer. Peel and mash to substitute, measuring out 28 ounces. You can always use fresh onions and jalapeño peppers as well.

PER SERVING

Calories:	18
Total Fat:	0.1 g
Cholesterol:	0 mg
Sodium:	346 mg
Carbohydrates:	4 g
Protein:	0.7 g

*See glossary for definition.

Avocado Salsa

Makes 12 servings

1 medium Spanish onion, finely chopped
2 large avocados, chopped
1 tablespoon lime juice
1 medium tomato, chopped
1 small hot chili pepper, chopped fine
2 tablespoons olive oil

1 teaspoon ground coriander
1 teaspoon ground cumin
1/4 teaspoon chili powder
3 tablespoons chopped fresh cilantro
4 drops hot sauce

MEXICO

In a medium bowl, place the chopped onion and avocado. Pour lime juice over onion and avocado; toss gently. Add chopped tomato; stir gently.

In a small skillet over medium heat, stir coriander, cumin, and chili powder in oil for one minute to enhance the flavors. When cool, add seasonings and hot sauce to the avocado mixture, gently stirring from the bottom up. Refrigerate until ready to serve, or serve warm.

PER SERVING

Calories:	84
Total Fat:	7 g
Cholesterol:	0 mg
Sodium:	6 mg
Carbohydrates:	5 g
Protein:	1 g

TEX-MEX

Debby's Fresh Salsa

Makes 8 servings

1 medium onion, sliced
2 medium tomatoes, quartered and sliced
1 cup cilantro, loosely packed
1/4 teaspoon salt
Juice of one lemon

In a food processor, process onion until chopped. Add tomatoes and cilantro; process only until tomatoes are chopped. Pour into a bowl; sprinkle with salt. Add lemon juice. Stir and serve.

SERVING SUGGESTION: This is good with any recipe in the book that calls for salsa. It is especially good with the Chicken Fajitas (p.97).

PER SERVING

Calories:	33
Total Fat:	0.3 g
Cholesterol:	0 mg
Sodium:	78 mg
Carbohydrates:	8 g
Protein:	1 g

Eggplant Dip [Baba Gannoujh (bah·bah gah·NOOSH)]

Makes 10 servings

2 small eggplants, halved lengthwise
2 cloves garlic
2 tablespoons fresh lemon juice
3 tablespoons tahini*
1 tablespoon olive oil
Salt to taste

Preheat oven to 375°F. Sprinkle halved eggplant flesh with salt. Let sit for 15 minutes; rinse. Pat dry with paper towel. Place eggplants, flesh-side up, on a baking sheet; bake for 20 minutes. Remove from oven; remove skins.

In a food processor or blender, process eggplant flesh, garlic, lemon juice, tahini, and olive oil until mixture reaches a dip consistency. Season to taste with salt.

This is a favorite appetizer in the Middle East and will keep in the refrigerator.

SERVING SUGGESTION: Serve with pita bread or regular bread.

*See glossary for definition.

A TASTE OF THE MIDDLE EAST

PER SERVING

Calories:	64
Total Fat:	4 g
Cholesterol:	0 mg
Sodium:	3 mg
Carbohydrates:	7 g
Protein:	2 g

SWITZERLAND

Fondue

Makes 40 servings

1 pound Swiss cheese, shredded
3 tablespoons cornstarch
1/2 teaspoon salt
1/4 teaspoon white pepper

1/4 teaspoon nutmeg
2 cups buttermilk
1 clove garlic

In a large bowl, combine cheese, cornstarch, salt, pepper, and nutmeg. Set aside.

In a fondue pot or chafing dish over low heat, heat buttermilk and garlic clove. When hot, remove garlic; add cheese mixture. Stir occasionally until cheese is melted. Serve from fondue pot or chafing dish.

SERVING SUGGESTION: Have a fondue party. Give each person a long fondue fork. Place pieces of French, Italian, sourdough, or Russian bread—or chunks of vegetables—onto the forks. (Use your imagination!) Then, dunk whatever is on the fork into the fondue. *Scrumptious!*

PER SERVING

Calories:	50
Total Fat:	3 g
Cholesterol:	11 mg
Sodium:	69 mg
Carbohydrates:	2 g
Protein:	4 g

Hummus

Makes 20 servings

2 16-ounce cans garbanzo beans,
    drained—reserve liquid
4 tablespoons fresh lemon juice
3 tablespoons olive oil

4 cloves garlic
1/2 teaspoon salt
1/4 teaspoon paprika
1/3 cup tahini*

**A TASTE OF THE
MIDDLE EAST**

In a blender, puree all ingredients at high speed. Use some of the reserved garbanzo liquid if mixture is too thick. It should be a smooth paste when finished.

SERVING SUGGESTION: Use in sandwiches and as a dip for vegetables or crackers.

PER SERVING

Calories:	97
Total Fat:	4 g
Cholesterol:	0 mg
Sodium:	243 mg
Carbohydrates:	12 g
Protein:	3 g

*See glossary for definition.

**A TASTE OF
LATIN AMERICA**

Snappy Salsa Dip

Makes 8 servings

1 8-ounce package fat-free cream cheese, softened
1/2 cup salsa

In a medium mixing bowl, mix softened cream cheese and salsa. Store in refrigerator until ready to use.

SERVING SUGGESTION: Use in place of mayonnaise, as a cracker spread, or as a vegetable dip. The uses are limitless, and fat free!

PER SERVING
Calories: 31
Total Fat: 0.4 g
Cholesterol: 2 mg
Sodium: 196 mg
Carbohydrates: 2 g
Protein: 4 g

Yogurt Dip

Makes 8 servings

1 teaspoon cumin seed
1 cup plain nonfat yogurt
1 small red chili, seeded and minced
1/2 teaspoon paprika
2 tablespoons chopped fresh mint
1 tablespoon chopped fresh cilantro

A TASTE OF THE MIDDLE EAST

In a small skillet over medium heat, cook cumin seeds for 2 minutes or until fragrant. Remove from heat; cool.

In a medium bowl, combine all ingredients and stir. Refrigerate until ready to serve.

SERVING SUGGESTION: This is great to serve with anything spicy. Asians would put it this way: "It is something coolly to serve with something heaty."

PER SERVING

Calories:	18
Total Fat:	0.1 g
Cholesterol:	1 mg
Sodium:	23 mg
Carbohydrates:	2 g
Protein:	2 g

ISRAEL

Mushroom-Walnut Spread

Makes 24 servings

2 tablespoons olive oil
1/2 pound mushrooms, cleaned and sliced
1 small onion, quartered
1 cup chopped walnuts
2 cloves garlic
Salt to taste

In a medium skillet over medium-high heat, sauté mushrooms in olive oil until tender.

In a food processor or blender, process onion, nuts, garlic, and sautéed mushrooms till smooth. Season to taste.

SERVING SUGGESTION: Serve with crackers or Challah (p. 31).

This is a Jewish Passover side dish they call "liver paté." Very tasty!

PER SERVING
Calories:	51
Total Fat:	4 g
Cholesterol:	0 mg
Sodium:	1 mg
Carbohydrates:	2 g
Protein:	1 g

Roasted Red Pepper Spread

Makes 12 servings

1 8-ounce package light cream cheese
1 cup roasted red peppers*
3/4 teaspoon garlic powder
2 tablespoons chopped fresh basil
2 tablespoons red wine vinegar
1 tablespoon evaporated milk

ITALY

In your food processor**, process all ingredients until almost smooth. Keep refrigerated until ready to serve.

SERVING SUGGESTION: Serve with crackers, fresh vegetables, or French bread. Use in place of mayonnaise on your sandwiches.

*To roast peppers, quarter the peppers and remove the stalk, seeds, and membranes. Place on a cookie sheet under the broiler, skin side up, until charred and blistered. (Watch carefully that they don't burn.) Remove from heat, rub away the skins, and chop.

Though fresh is usually better, you can purchase roasted red peppers at the grocery store. You will find them in jars near the olives and pickles.

**If you don't have a food processor, pulsing in a blender will do, but watch that you don't do it too long.

PER SERVING

Calories:	49
Total Fat:	3 g
Cholesterol:	11 mg
Sodium:	108 mg
Carbohydrates:	2 g
Protein:	2 g

HAWAII, USA

Apricot Barbecue Sauce

BERT LEAHEY

Makes 10 servings

1/4 cup canola oil
1/4 cup white vinegar
3/4 cup apricot jam
1/2 cup catsup

1/2 teaspoon salt
2 tablespoons brown sugar
1/2 teaspoon dried oregano
2 tablespoons sliced green onions

In a medium saucepan over medium-high heat, combine all ingredients; bring to a boil. Remove from heat.

SERVING SUGGESTION: This sauce can be used in place of many gravies and sauces that accompany entrées.

PER SERVING

Calories:	130
Total Fat:	5 g
Cholesterol:	0 mg
Sodium:	260 mg
Carbohydrates:	22 g
Protein:	0.4 g

Glossary

Asiago cheese (ah·SYAH·goh)
An aged Italian cheese with a rich, nutty flavor; similar to Parmegiano. It's a hard cheese suitable for grating and can be found in the deli section of most supermarkets.

Chiles de arbol
Also known as chili flakes, these peppers are readily available crushed; you may have seen them at pizza restaurants in shaker jars. Chili flakes are available in the seasonings section of your local supermarket.

Clotted cream
This specialty of Devonshire, England is made by gently heating unpasteurized milk until a layer of cream forms on the surface. The thickened cream is then removed. The traditional English "cream tea" consists of clotted cream and jam served with scones and tea. Clotted cream can be found in gourmet markets and specialty stores.

Feta cheese (FEHT·uh)
This classic Greek cheese is traditionally made of sheep's or goat's milk and has a rich, tangy flavor. It can be found in square cakes or pre-crumbled in the deli section of your local supermarket.

Ghee
Clarified butter that has been taken a step further by simmering it until all the moisture evaporates and the milk solids begin to brown, giving the butter a nutty, caramellike flavor and aroma. This step also gives ghee a high smoke point—almost 375°F. Ghee can be found in Middle Eastern and gourmet markets.

Jícama (HEE·kah·mah)
This bulbous root vegetable has a sweet, nutty flavor and is good both raw and cooked. The skin should be removed just prior to use. Jícama is available November through May and can be found in the produce section of most supermarkets.

Julienne (joo·lee·EHN)
To julienne is to cut into thin, matchstick-like strips. First slice the vegetable (or fruit, etc.) into 1/8"-thick slices; then stack those and cut into 1/8"-thick strips.

Marzipan
A pliable mixture of almond paste and sugar; it can be found in the baking section of your local supermarket.

Mortar and pestle (MOR·tuhr / PEHS·tl)
A mortar is a bowl-shaped container and a pestle is a rounded, batlike instrument used for grinding spices, herbs, and other foods. Mortar and pestle sets can be found in kitchen supply and specialty stores.

Phyllo (FEE·loh)
Tissue-thin layers of pastry dough that are packaged and frozen; phyllo dough is readily available in most supermarkets.

Pine nut [*In.* pignolia (pee·YOH·lee·ah)]
These high-fat nuts are actually inside the pine cone, which generally must be heated to facilitate their removal. This labor-intensive process is what makes these nuts so expensive. They can be purchased in bulk or packaged in most supermarkets.

Portobello mushroom (por·toh·BEHL·loh)
A very large mushroom—the fully mature crimino, which is a variation of the common white mushroom. It has an open, flat cap with a dense, meaty texture; the stems are very woody and should be removed. Portobellos can be found in gourmet markets as well as many supermarkets.

Rice sticks
Rice sticks generally refer to rice-flour noodles. They can be found in Asian markets or the international foods section of your grocery store.

Roma tomatoes
Oval-shaped tomatoes that can be found in the produce section of your supermarket.

Tahini (tah·HEE·nee)
A paste made from ground toasted sesame seeds that can be found with the peanut butter in most supermarkets.

Watercress
Watercress has small, crisp, dark green leaves. Its flavor is slightly bitter with a peppery snap. Watercress is available year-round and is sold in small bouquets—choose crisp leaves with a deep, vibrant color.

Zest
The perfumy outermost rind layer of citrus fruit which is removed with the aid of a citrus zester, paring knife, or fine grater. Only the colored portion of the rind (and not the white pith) is considered the zest.

Index

Breads

Banana Scones .25
Breakfast Muffins 24
Challah 31
Chapatis 27
English Muffin Loaf 32
Focaccia 33
Green Chili & Onion Bread 34
Naan 28
Pita Bread 29
Scones 26
Spicy Corn Pudding Bread 35
Torte Rustica .36

Desserts

Cakes

Banana German Chocolate Cake 126
Pastel de Piña 128
German Chocolate Cake 127
Rice Cake 129

Cookies

Butter Cookies 118
Chinese Almond Cookies 119
Chinese New Year Cookies 120
Chocolate-filled Bonbons 122
Dutch Bon Ket 123
Fortune Cookies 124

Miscellaneous desserts

Bavarian Honey Lemon Pudding 132
Crème Brûlée 133
Flan 134
Funnel Cakes 125
Leopard-Spots Ice Cream 135
Pavlova 136
Raspberry Kissel 137
Sesame Honey Bars 117

Pies

Italian Prune Pie 130
Swedish Apple Pie 131

Drinks

Blended frozen drinks

Banana-Grape Smoothie 22
Frosty Yogurt Drink 20

Mango Lassi .18
Seth's Orange Sensation 21
Sweet Lassi 19

Cold drinks

Fruit Cooler 8
Lemon & Lime Barley Water 11
Orange Cooler 9
Raspberry Lemonade Cooler 10

Hot drinks

Christmas Wassail 12
Curried Tomato Juice 13
French Hot Chocolate 14
Glögg 15
Russian Tea .16
Spiced Tea 17

Entrees

"Finger foods"

African Bean Burritos 56
Chinese Spring Rolls 54
Cornmeal Tarts 57
Kabobs 53
Mediterranean Pita Rounds 60
Nimikies 59

Samosas 58

Sfeeha 61

Vietnamese Spring Rolls 55

Casseroles and the like

Chicken Casserole Mexicali 70

Chicken Kiev 71

Chicken Morengo 72

Corn Tortilla Casserole 73

Enchiladas 67

Hong Kong Casserole 74

Indian Nut Loaf 76

Manicotti .75

"Nine Bean Loaf®" 78

Spinach Pie 79

Stuffed Cabbage Leaves 68

Veranike 69

Miscellaneous entrees

Chicken Fajitas 97

Chiles Relleños 64

Ecuadorian Rice Omelet 65

Egg Foo Yong 66

Haystacks .98

Salsa-topped Potatoes 99

Sausage & Tortellini Pasta 80

Tagliatelle .81

Patties and the like

Falafels 62

Tofu Patties 63

Rice & beans

Chik Fried Rice 91

Cuban Black Beans 94

Pinto Beans 96

Spanish Rice I 92

Spanish Rice II 93

"Served over rice"

Curry 86

Garbanzo Curry 87

Lemon-Apricot Chicken 82

Pineapple Sweet & Sour *Skallops®* I . . .83

Pineapple Sweet & Sour *Skallops®* II . . .84

Spicy Vegetable Dahl 89

Teriyaki Tofu 85

Thai Tofu Curry 88

Tofu Etouffee 90

Miscellaneous

Dips

Avocado Salsa 145

Debby's Fresh Salsa 146

Eggplant Dip 147

Fondue .148

Hummus 149

Snappy Salsa Dip 150

Yogurt Dip 151

Sauces

Apricot Barbeque Sauce 154

Chirmol Sauce 144

Soups

Corn Soup 139

Finnish Vegetable Soup 140

Refried Bean Soup 141

Roman Holiday Soup 142

Tortellini & Bean Soup 143

Spreads

Mushroom-Walnut Spread 152

Roasted Red Pepper Spread 153

Soybean Mayonnaise 75

Salads

Chinese Cabbage Salad 42

Cranberry Salad 50

Cucumber & Tomato Salad 45

Fruit Salad 51

Greek Spinach Salad 39

Lentil Salad .46

Mandarin Spinach Salad 40

Radish Salad 47

Sesame Angel Hair Salad 43

Sesame Chicken Noodle Salad 48

Swedish Beet Salad 44

Toasted Bread Salad 49

Watercress Salad 41

Vegetables

Cajun Potato Wedges 101

Carrots With Cilantro 102

Carrottes au Cumin 103

Choclo Espanjosa 104

Mexican Hominy 106

Onion Pie 105

Pancit Bijon 108

Peppery Green Beans 109

Potato Curry 110

Spinach Sauce 111

Sweet Corn Cakes 112

Swiss Eggplant 113

Teriyaki Eggplant Cutlets 114

Zucchini Casserole 115

Commercial Product Index

• •

Loma Linda®

Linkettes®: Spanish Rice II 93

Tender Bits: Mandarin Spinach Salad 40

Vege-Burger®: Sfeeha 61

    Stuffed Cabbage Leaves 68

Morningstar Farms®

Grillers®: Salsa-topped Potatoes 99

Scramblers®: Chik Fried Rice 91

    Ecuadorian Rice Omelet 65

    Egg Foo Yong 66

Flan 134

Teriyaki Eggplant Cutlets 114

Zucchini Casserole 115

Breakfast Patties:

    Sausage & Tortellini Pasta 80

Natural Touch®

Nine Bean Loaf® 78

Worthington®

Chic-Kettes®: Kabobs 53

Chili: Haystacks 98

Diced Chik: Chik Fried Rice 91

FriChik®:

    Chicken Casserole Mexicali 70

Chicken Fajitas 97

Chicken Kiev 71

Chicken Morengo 72

Egg Foo Yong 66

Lemon-Apricot Chicken 82

Sesame Chicken Noodle Salad 48

Meatless Salami (frozen): Torte Rustica . .36

Meatless Smoked Turkey (frozen):

    Chinese Spring Rolls 54

Multigrain Cutlets®:

    Hong Kong Casserole 74

Vegetable Skallops®

    Pineapple Sweet & Sour Skallops® I . . .83

    Pineapple Sweet & Sour Skallops® II . .84